THE
SEVEN
PRINCIPLES

Toward a Life of
Meaning and Purpose

Editor: Reb Matisyahu Brown

Editor: Reb Eden Pearlstein

Cover and book design: RP Design and Development

Toward a Life of
Meaning and Purpose

THE SEVEN
PRINCIPLES

THIS BOOK IS DEDICATED
IN HONOR OF

MR. LEWIS TOPPER שיחי׳

FIRST EDITION DEDICATION:

In honor and in memory of
Stephen Matthew Appel ע״ה
Who gave our family a purpose for living.
In honor of the gift of love he gave us all.

The Appel Family

OPENING:
A WORLD OF HOPE

W E DESPERATELY SEEK CERTAINTIES in a world plagued with uncertainties. In a world steeped in ambiguity, we yearn for clarity. Surrounded by corruption and superficiality, we all deeply long for integrity, authenticity and sacredness.

In the name of advancement and enlightenment, human beings have formed a world in which almost nothing is sacred anymore, a world in which ideologies triumph over humanity. And what is the dominant, most lauded ideology of them all? Relativism. When everything is relative, nothing is really relevant. When everything goes, nothing really matters. It is a world where there are no absolutes, and essentially no clear distinctions between what is good and what is really evil, between what is noble and what is lowly, and what is 'worth fighting for' and what is 'not worth a minute of my time'.

In an effort to be completely non-judgmental, our culture has lost its very sense of all judgment. Although being non-judgmental is positive in essence, making it into a rigid ideology unveils its negative flip side. One begins to condone harmful and traumatizing acts in the name of absolute openness to diverse perspectives.

Human beings seem to have also lost their way and moral compass, despite all our advancements in science, medicine and technology. Studies and advancements in the areas of human consciousness and life-giving practices seem to be lagging far behind all 'external' advances. As a result, reverence has become irrelevant. This is because in the name of 'freedom', 'success', 'security' or 'pleasure', all norms can be collapsed — nothing is sacred any longer, nothing is worth upholding, and no one is to be emulated. But in a world where everything is 'OK', nothing is actually 'OK'.

When all is said and done, the only thing that most people really value and revere is their own ego, their self-centered 'i'. Despite their belief in relativism, their comforts and ability to attract the admiration of others somehow rise above all other considerations in life. 'Yes,' one might agree, 'in this world no one amounts to anything... except for me; i am important, and my friends, my family, my culture, my politics, my public image, my beauty, my career, my property, my feelings, my longevity....

In truth, the celebration of 'me' is not automatically bad; the real negativity arises when it implies the exclusion of 'you'. There is no longer any sense of 'we'; there is no grand vision or dream for humanity, just thinly cloaked greed and conflict with others. Indeed, when the 'i' dominates our world-view, there is a total eclipse of authentic spirituality, soul, and moral obligation towards others. Life, from this narrow, self-serving perspective, gradually leads to an endless cycle of dissatisfaction, greed, addiction, brutality, trauma, and ever greater despair and bitter dissatisfaction.

A person's selfish 'i-ness' whispers to him that it will obtain happiness for him, but it never produces more than a brief illusion of happiness or a very temporary state of contentment. As one debases himself, following the dictates of the urge for self-gratification, one gradually begins to feel worthless and eventually hopeless, living without vision and patience for what is truly fulfilling. As one continues down this endless path of temporary fulfillment, the discontent and emptiness drives the compulsion to stuff oneself again and again, only to feel even more empty each time. One sells their heart, intellect, and soul at a deep discount and then becomes so famished that they will gorge themselves on emptiness and waste.

When people postpone or simply disregard deeper meaning and higher purpose, they are left alienated, unhappy and hungry. This has been demonstrated time and time again by the triumph of political movements and the establishment of man-made societal systems, which all promise security or a good life, but end in further desolation. Modern technology and social media also promise us a good life of connection with others, but the deeper one involves himself in them, the more disconnected, lonely, alienated and lost they can become. When people actively attempt to replace the deeper joy of living for a higher purpose with a trivial or temporary sense of security or pleasure, they ultimately destroy their lives and the lives of others.

Even if a society's values were centered on something seemingly noble, such as technical and scientific knowledge and an understanding of the physical universe, the eventual result would be a society of apathetic, uninspired people. Such values would drain people of wonder and awe, causing them to roam aimlessly through life. For if the basic physical principles of the universe ultimately suggest that everything is relative, then what really matters? Then, what are love, compassion and happiness, but neurochemical reactions? What are other people but stepping stones to greater achievement? What is life but a vicious competition to attain ever-elusive goals?

If a discovery of the vastness of the universe does not inspire wonder, but rather the urge to grab for more power, profit or pleasure, that vastness does not make us bigger. On the contrary, it can shrink us down until we ask the deadly question, 'What is life really worth?' On the scale of even small galaxies, one is not even a speck, one is nothing, invisible, without a shred of significance.

The aim and prayer of this text is to help restore meaning, purpose, values, awe and wonder to the reader's life. Here are the eternal unchanging spiritual, moral and ethical principles at the depths of life, which allow people to live with genuine happiness, with authentic connection to others, with soulful awareness of the Creator, and with the ability to cultivate true, lasting success, pleasure and contentment. These principles allow humanity to share this beautiful world in harmony and moral clarity.

HOW WE MEASURE TIME

Ancient human beings observed the seasonal cycles of nature and surmised that all of life and all of reality is cyclical; there are just bigger and smaller cycles of time and rhythmic fluctuation. They understood time not as progressive flow towards a destination, rather as a closed circuit in which everything repeatedly resets to zero and thus remains essentially the same. There may be ups and downs, a little forward and back, but ultimately nothing progresses; the world and all its beings must forever live out a predictable replay loop of the past.

If there is no destination for history, there can be no real directionality or trajectory at any phase. There also cannot be a real 'beginning' or a real sense of purpose in Creation. In a beginningless, endless universe, every image has already appeared, every 'accomplishment' is merely a copy of the past, and there is nothing new. In this worldview, people have no ability to begin afresh, no freedom to choose a new path. Without a progressive movement of the cosmos, there is no possibility for personal growth as well as collective evolution. The conditions into which a person is born, from their social stature to his genetic makeup, from his astrological constellation to his 'personal interests', are automatic and forever fixed and sealed. In fact, there are no actual 'personal interests', for each person is a no more than a culturally defined and predetermined role.

The ancients believed in a world dominated by fate; if you were born a slave, for example, your fate was to be a slave, and you could never change that fact and become a free person. If you were born into a lower caste, you and your offspring would forever remain in that caste.

Observing the forces of the natural world, the ancients also perceived the power of storms, lightning, rain, heat, fertility, death, and so forth, and surmised that each of these many forces had autonomy and 'personal' agency. In this way, the world was full of different deities who were constantly engaging in conflicts and wars for dominance. 'Fate' would always gain the upper hand and the stronger deity would prevail — until the next cycle and the next repetition of the battle.

Just as their pantheon of deities was a rigid hierarchy, so was their society and family. For example, the oldest child in a family was always favored, even despite a lack of merit. In such a world, it was virtually impossible for a slave to even dream of being a free person, or a 'lower class' person to imagine rising out of poverty and oppression. There was no room for personal transformation, nor the experience of miracles or true acts of compassion. Human life was felt to be mechanical, conforming to rigid formulae.

FATE VERSES FAITH

Ancient civilization was entirely entangled within the worldview of mythology. The basic premise of mythology and its warring deities implied inevitable tragedy. Despite the intense dramas of each force attempting to outwit the other, any 'victory' was forfeited, since in the end everything simply went back to the way it was before.

This is the way people felt about themselves as well, as mythology is nothing more than an expression of a deeper psyche, a 'collective unconscious' expressed in symbolic forms. Just as life was seen as a closed system, it wouldn't matter how much you struggled against your nature, your environment or your predicament. Even if you were temporarily victorious, at the end of the day, everything just reverts to how it began. As there is no real change or progress, the hero's journey thus always ends in loss.

From this perspective, life itself is a great tragedy; we can try to work against fate, but in the end, fate always wins. At birth, your life is already set. Some people may feel the urge to make a difference, to better themselves or to do something beyond what is expected or accepted, but they inexorably fail. There is thus no way out of a fixed system. Greek tragedy is an aesthetic ritual that grew out of ancient mythology. The Greeks believed in moria or anake, simply translated means 'blind fate'. The hero, who wishes to journey away from his assumed fate, always fails.

In this conception of the universe there is no essential goodness to life, only an endless and inevitable cycle of struggle, tragedy and death. It tries to tell you that you are doomed from the beginning, that negative traits cannot be overcome — your genetics, your upbringing, your social class dictates who you are and who you will be; your destiny is locked in; the world as a whole, as well, cannot get any worse, but nor can it get better.

WITHOUT INDIVIDUALITY

To the ancients, only the highest echelon of society really 'mattered' and only its members had some sense of individuality, while the lower rungs, virtually everyone, existed only to serve the higher echelon and the king, whom they believed to be a 'divine incarnate'.

In such a devastating worldview, one is not an individual, just a cog in a great wheel of life. A person has no real worth nor does a higher collective purpose exist. There is no hope or possibility for redemption, no dreaming or aspiring for another kind of life. At the basis of all experience is hopelessness and lifelessness.

Sadly, in our postmodern world, this fatalistic type of thinking has somewhat returned. With the collapse of a sense of absolute truth and absolute morality, nothing can be defined and there is no room for real movement to happen, as there is no place to go. There is no good or bad; everything is like a circle, with no 'up' or 'down'. Although the culture is focused on service of the self, there is ultimately no significance to any individual. Virtually every 'hero', even when they are worshiped by some, will be scorned or discredited by many others. All values are denied in the nihilistic worldview, so there can be no progress or building of value. Everyone, in the end, returns to 'zero'.

In this paradigm, there is no ultimate goal or aspiration in life; one can only hope to work hard enough to occasionally have a good time, to eat and drink and engage in a hobby, to try and sweep their suffering under the rug, and then return to work to fund the next cycle of gratification. As everything is seen as relative, everything can be refuted and discarded. In the grips of this worldview, most postmodern people don't honestly feel that anything really matters. At the base of this psychology, there is an inner wasteland of apathy, indifference, and hopelessness.

A WORLD OF POSSIBILITY

Here is where the gift of the Torah comes in with a vision of renewal and real progress, and its path of hope and the preciousness of human life. The Torah reveals that there is a beginning: "In the beginning, G-d created the Heavens and the Earth." Such opens the Book of Genesis, the foundation of faith. "In the beginning and for the intentions of beginnings. Life is not merely a beginning-less, static circle. And since there is an intentional beginning, there will also be an intentional end or goal; the world will progress and eventually there will be a complete redemption of all beings.

When we believe that if we were not successful yesterday, we cannot make a new "beginning" and be more successful today, then our past 'imprisons' our present. In this state of 'exile' or constricted consciousness, change is never a possibility and any real movement is unattainable. Sadly, living this way, the future is already closed in front of us.

Genesis brings us a positive, empowering and holy path of being new every day and ultimately every moment. We are enabled to take full responsibility for our past, yet be fully in the moment with an open door to the future. We have the conviction that we can start over again and begin anew at any juncture. We are never defined by our past, nor pulled into a pre-defined future.

There is an undeniable cyclical pattern to nature and the seasons, yet, even this circle turns within an overall linear progression forward or upward. In other words, from the perspective of Torah, life is like a spiral. Even as we live through cycles of time — evening, morning, afternoon, fall, winter, spring, summer — we are simultaneously revisiting the past, 'beginning anew' and climbing higher and higher toward a final redemption.

As many ancient people perceived and celebrated, the Presence of the Creator of Life can be found within the natural world, and they thanked the Divine life force for the rain, the soil, and the new harvest. Genesis revealed that the Divine Presence is also found in time and in the trajectory of history. Sacredness can be encountered not only in objects and space, but within the rhythms of time. In fact, time was created as the foundation of space.

History continues moving forward, as time itself is progressive by nature, flowing from a primordial act of creation (past), traversing a period of struggle and clarification (present), and finally resolving in a great homecoming of all beings (future).

It is vital to realize that the world is actually getting better and moving toward a state of inclusive Unity. Despite appearances of increasing negativity, spiritual pollution and hardship, as explored above — as we spiral toward redemption, humanity is gradually learning from its mistakes and letting go of barbarism, idolatry, hopelessness and moral depravity. More and more people are trading fatalistic and reactive thinking for deeper awakening in the Oneness of the Creator. They are enthusiastically embracing practical Divine principles for nurturing a meaningful, beneficial life, and beginning to experience inner freedom even within the limitations of their outer life. Whether we can see it or not, each of us as individuals are progressing, emotionally, mentally and existentially. Our lives are part of the plan of the great homecoming. Our souls are learning from our mistakes and we are gathering strength for a global spiritual breakthrough. The fact that you are reading this book is proof of this.

Indeed, 'faith' will eventually triumph over 'fate', whether this comes about through our collective choice or by some sort of Divine push. Such a push can come to the world by means of difficult obstacles or through the spontaneous opening of inner wellsprings of joy, but it is preferable that we actively choose faith, rather than it being thrust upon us.

Resolute faith, and actions that flow from faith, can overcome all apparent obstacles. Just because a person was born poor, disabled or uneducated does not mean that limitation is their lot. Just because one came from a materially or spiritually low condition does not mean they cannot rise to the greatest heights, physically, financially, mentally, emotionally and spiritually.

More than 4,000 years ago, Abraham and Sarah lived in an area surrounded by idolatrous denigration of life. Yet, they had the great courage to listen to the call of the one true Divinity and leave that place behind. This was the beginning of their career of reaching out with kindness to everyone they met and teaching others about Monotheism and a life of ethics and purpose.

We always have the ability to take the true 'hero's journey'. Like Abraham and Sarah, we can journey forth from our comfort zone, from the confines of our birthplace, upbringing and genetics, and carve out a higher level of life for ourselves and our families. We all have the innate, spiritual potential for movement and genuine change; we all have an ability to grow, to learn, to let go of others' fixed perceptions of who we can be. We are all capable of deciding to be true to ourselves.

We all are charged to heed this calling to take our own journey. We can rise up and become our true potential. We can decide that we will not allow the 'stars' or the circumstances of our birth and upbringing, our education, financial status or surrounding culture, to dictate how we are going to live our lives. We are built with the ability to strive for personal redemption and inner freedom. We have the keys to faith, the keys to transcending the world of tragedy and inevitable fate. What's more, whenever we seem to fall from our path of growth, we can immediately get up and return to it, and continue our journey right where we left off.

As life is linear and flexible, rather than static and fixed, we are not stuck and we are not boxed in by our past mistakes, nor by anyone's negative predictions of what we can reach in life. We are not limited by 'astrology', 'psychology', 'genetics', or personal history. We have the ability to be unaffected by our environment and past, and to actively grow, move, journey, and progress. We can be open to the 'surprise' of life, to dreaming, hoping, and having faith in the future. Time moves forward and so can we.

This tremendously positive worldview is part of the redemptive wisdom that the Torah gifted to the world. No longer is humanity lacking a universal guide to becoming free from brutality, idolatry, mythology, determinism and nihilistic relativism. With the revelation of the Torah, every human being is fully empowered to choose a meaningful, fulfilling life. The seven liberative principles that will be unwrapped in the coming chapters are sparkling gems from the

Torah's treasury of wisdom, which can guide anyone to great spiritual prosperity.

EVERY INDIVIDUAL MATTERS

In the Torah's revelation of the Uniqueness and Singularity of the Creator, the uniqueness and singularity of human beings was also revealed. Each individual person is created in the Divine image, and is therefore special and unlike any other. Even genetically identical twins have different fingerprints. Each person has an irreplaceable relationship with the Divine; each is singularly important and valuable.

As a result, no individual person can rightly be substituted, pushed aside or sacrificed for the wellbeing of a collective or society. Say, for example, if bandits surround a town and they announce that the townspeople must hand over a certain innocent person to be killed, otherwise they will wipe out the entire town, Torah wisdom asserts that the community is not allowed to hand over that person or force him to sacrifice himself. He can choose to do so to save the collective, however they cannot take away his personal sovereignty. No one can be sacrificed for the greater good of the world because each person is like the entire world, each is singularly cherished.

Every life is essential — we are not just a part of a collective. Each human being is to be honored and celebrated for who they are, for each contains the image of the One Divinity. To respect a person is to respect the Divinity within them.

In fact, a spark of Divine lifeforce enlivens every creature — every animal, insect, plant, and mineral. Everything in the world has been created with a specific Divine intention and thus everything has meaning, purpose and a destiny. On a deeper level, the great purpose and destiny of Creation is brought closer through every thought, word and action of each individual person. Everything and everyone, at every moment, is contributing to the redemption of all.

This is because every individual, with all of his or her unique qualities, desires and quests, is an expression of the Singularity of the Creator, and all are equally valuable. In our era, the truth that "all persons are created equal" may be self-evident to most of us — but this is only so because the wisdom teachings of the Torah have become universal. Such a truth would have sounded absurd to many ancient thinkers. The notion that every human being and each creature must be respected and revered for its unique and infinite value, would have seemed nonsensical to the rigidly hierarchical cultures of the past. The Torah brought a revolution in consciousness, a revolution that is still unfolding. Everyone who embraces the principles of this consciousness is accelerating the redemption of all life.

The redemption and liberation offered by the Torah is a return to a sense of reverence, a sacredness of self and others and all of life. Each person will actively return to a life of compassion and valuing others. In the redeemed world envisioned by Torah, no one will hurt another human being, and will eventually refrain from inflicting unnecessary pain upon any living being. All will respect the belongings and feelings of others, with a deep sense of healthy boundaries and generosity. What belongs to another is part of their sacred life; fully redeemed people do not desire what belongs to another, for they are deeply satisfied with the Divine life and abundance flowing through their own being. A world culture of contentment will feel like Heaven on earth. Each person has a role to play in co-creating this new world.

OPTIMISM

The truth is, the universe is continuously unfolding towards its ultimate destiny, whether humans choose to help and assist in this progressive unfolding, or Heaven forbid, they choose the path of self-destruction and harm to others. Either way, in the grand scheme of things, history keeps marching forward toward its revelation of pervasive value and goodness. Knowing this is radically optimistic, however such optimism is not a luxury or a folly — it is a fact of life, the nature of existence. Life, by nature, moves ever forward toward its culmination in complete positivity and fulfilment.

Still, even though there is no escaping life's evolution into universal compassion and goodness, we can only truly resonate with this great future and help hasten its arrival — and begin to experience its dawning in the present — when we practice the principles revealed by the Torah. The first step, however, is to adopt the radical optimism of the Torah's view, including an inevitable culmination in world redemption. Then practice can follow.

We also need to fight our subtle intellectual snobbery against such deep optimism. Since the so-called 'Enlightenment' it has become fashionable for intellectuals to raise a banner of cynicism, nihilism, and pessimism, while belief in progress and fundamental goodness is left to romantic poets and utopian dreamers. To the 'realist' and the intellectual, deeply optimistic beliefs and purely positive action seem naive and superficial.

Yet, pessimism's destination is despondency and hopelessness, for in this view, every mistake and misfortune is permanent. 'It's always like this', one asserts, 'suffering is inevitable,' or 'I am a bad person; I cannot possibly make the world a better place.' Accordingly, the path of returning to a life of sacredness and honor seems impossible. In a traditional elaboration of the story in Genesis, after Cain killed his brother Abel, his father, Adam, asked Cain, "What was the consequence of your act?" Cain answered, "I returned whole-heartedly to a life of goodness, and the full impact of my mistake did not come to me." "Such is the power of return?" Adam exclaimed. "I did not realize that by 'returning', a person's past misdeeds are erased completely and considered by the Creator as if they had never taken place!" Adam thought he had been forever banished from the goodness of life and could do nothing about it. When he began to embrace the deep optimism he learned from his son, he realized that one day, human beings might even 'return' to the state of innocence, freedom and satisfaction that he experienced in the Garden of Eden. He realized that redemption is possible.

To be optimistic is to view mistakes and misfortunes as temporary, as exceptions, and even as important moments of learning or crouching down to arise higher and stronger than ever before. In fact, there is no word for 'sin' in the Torah — the Hebrew word cheit really means 'to miss the goal'. Say we have a goal in mind of studying self-development for 15 minutes a day. If by the end of the day we missed that goal, it doesn't mean we cannot return to the goal and start anew tomorrow, or perhaps even meet the goal today. In fact, we can use this omission as a lesson in self-development, and find a positive way to ensure success in the future. To live a healthy, happy productive life, we need to let go of the narrative that 'it is always bad,' or 'I cannot," to unlearn the pessimistic ideas we have been taught, and to embrace the path of positive growth.

Part of our un-learning is actually fighting for optimism. In this context, 'fighting' means doing more than simply sitting down and finding reasons to be optimistic that things will change. It means recognizing our power to actively make things better. We are not just waiting passively for our lives and the world to eventually change for the better. We need to facilitate this change. We can get up and take an initiative and cause transformation in the sphere of our life. As a wise sage once said, "Even having faith requires faith." To have faith that the world can become a brighter, safer and happier place, and that I can contribute to that, necessitates having faith in ourselves that we can act in a way that makes a positive difference in our own life and surroundings. Faith is a preemptive

How do we build faith in ourselves? We begin again and again: we return when we fall, we simply choose to get up and go back to 'moving forward' with faith, hope and optimism. When we make a definitive choice to live with deep optimism, everything in life appears optimistic. We begin to see more and more opportunities to do good and enjoy being alive. We begin to stand in awe of all human beings, animals, vegetation and even inanimate forms. We come to life and embrace moments of wonder, openness, reverence… and joy.

Joy builds upon itself and it multiplies our strength to do good and experience the good. We find more and more reasons to be joyful and to bring joy to others. Whereas joy is not counted as one of the Seven Principles, it enables us to fulfill each of them. Joy is the preeminent spiritual weapon in our victory over negativity and exile. It is the only means to train our mind, heart and body to follow the guidance of our Creator, the Source of All Joy.

INTRODUCTION
THE SEVEN PRINCIPLES

H OW DO WE LIVE WITH A SENSE OF LOVE, passion, excitement, wonder, purpose and meaning — how do we open our eyes and behold the wonder of Creation, and the fullness, goodness and abundance available to us? We must develop a strong sense of the sacredness of our own life, and also recognize and respect the boundaries that our Creator wants us to maintain in reverence for the dignity of others' lives.

When we are not treating our fellow beings with respect, our minds and hearts become clogged with attitudes and feelings that alienate us from others, from ourselves and from our Divine Source. Subconscious regrets accumulate and we desensitize ourselves to the wonder, purpose and meaning. We distance ourselves from our own dignity.

CREATION REACHES REDEMPTION THROUGH REVELATION

If the creation of the world is intentional and it is progressing toward redemption, there must be a universal Divine communication inviting humanity to experience this progression. There must be a revelation that gives us the tools we need to contribute to it and accelerate it. If human life has a purpose, there must be a revelation of that purpose, and principles which allow us to live up to that purpose. In this way, revealed Divine laws and principles must be an inherent feature within Creation. No one can realistically achieve their purpose without an absolutely objective code or system of guidance. And this information cannot be absolutely objective if merely one individual received it in some form of private Divine encounter.

A revelation that is objective and relevant to all humanity demands transmission to the whole collective. This is the uniqueness of the cosmic, meta-historical, collective revelation at Mount Sinai — the revelation of Torah. Torah means "Teaching"; it is the complete system of guidance for life on earth, containing applications that are relevant for all historical eras, cultures and human circumstances.

Most spiritual traditions throughout history have been based on the claim of private Divine communication with a single person or a small group of elite figures. This scenario props the leaders up as intercessors, and construes blind belief in these people as the only means to access salvation. At Mount Sinai, by contrast, there was a collective, open-access revelation — three million devoted representatives of the human community experienced this unveiling of Divine Teaching simultaneously. Among them there was no disagreement regarding its veracity, objective meaning or practical import. This revelation was then transmitted from parents to children and teacher to students, in an unbroken, intimate chain, where it was constantly discussed, tested and verified in practice. In this collective receiving of revelation, seven universal principles of spiritual conduct and consciousness were indicated as expedient for all peoples and cultures, vital for hastening both individual self-development and a worldwide redemption.

The book in your hands is based on the covenant, which the Creator made with the entire human race after the world-cleansing Flood of Noah, marking the beginning of a 'new Creation' and a new level of collective maturity. This covenant is known as the Sheva Mitzvos B'nei Noach / 'Seven Directives for the Children of Noah'.

These seven eternal life principles are listed below in their simplest, abbreviated terms. Although they are expressed here in code form, on the surface appearing as simple 'rules' and 'do-nots', it is essential to know that each of them contain vast positive implications, and many layers of wisdom and life-affirming practical applications. It is not an exaggeration to state that these principles are the code for personal and global redemption.

In order to learn and remain aware of these principles at all times, and to begin training yourself to live in alignment to their deeper meanings, it would be effective at this point to write them out for yourself in their shortest form. It would also be helpful to start a dedicated journal with these seven points as a list of 'contents'. Perhaps write the principles out as a note that can be posted in a place where it will be seen and contemplated frequently. The act of writing the abbreviated principles by hand helps create neural pathways, inscribing them in your consciousness.

1) No idolatry

2) No blasphemy

3) No murder

4) No illicit relations

5) No stealing

6) No eating the limb of a living animal

7) Establish systems of justice.

In order to begin unpacking the deeper guidance and meaning behind these seven phrases, it is essential to add an initial layer of interpretation here. It is also vital to keep in mind that if we have made mistakes in any of these principles or their subtler implications, we can always 'return' — we can simply get back up, begin again, joyfully take up these principles again, and continue moving ourselves and our world forward toward fulfillment.

1) Refrain from worshiping any form, limitation, power, concept or idol — rather, do the opposite: rely fully on the One Source of Life, your loving and intimately caring Creator.

2) Refrain from "blaspheming" the Source of Life, rather to the opposite: 'bless' the Divine through expressions of gratitude

in thought, speech and action, and pray to Him.

3) Refrain from committing murder and enhance the lives of your fellow human beings. Remember that to save one life is like saving the entire world.

4) Refrain from engaging in any form of illicit relations; respect the sanctity of human relationships and promote a culture of noble love and dignity. Celebrate and nurture family life, as it is the bedrock of our future.

5) Refrain from stealing; live a life of giving, and be content with what you have.

6) Refrain from eating a limb torn from a living animal; show appropriate compassion to all creatures and minimize their pain. As the 'crown of creation', the final creature to be created and the most sophisticated and self-conscious, we human beings have a responsibility toward the welfare of all of the Creator's creation, animals and the whole planet.

7) Help to establish, or uphold, a system of authentic justice and charity; help others to act fairly and generously. Injustice in the world is our problem, and we are responsible to ensure that justice and righteousness prevails and there are unbiased judicial systems.

On the surface, these principles are self-explanatory, and most legal systems which allow for civility, property ownership, individual liberties and a generally open society, are founded upon them. After all, reasonably hospitable living conditions require that all members respect each other's lives and property; murder and theft are clearly violations of these foundations. Ensuring fairness is the only platform upon which a harmonious society can exist.

As these principles are logical and sensible, it may not seem necessary that they be transmitted to humanity as objective by their Creator. Yet if societies were to fulfill these laws merely because they 'make sense', then people would eventually change them so that they would make sense according to convenience or their current popular philosophy. What one society assumes is self-evident ethical behavior can seem foreign to another. People tend to bend ethical guidelines to fit their world-view, for instance, 'Killing is terrible, but this certainly doesn't apply to such-and-such group of people who are a burden and unworthy of living…'

Leaving absolute laws to man's own devices and ideologies can in fact lead him to think he is 'god' or a demigod. Nazi Germany and Stalinist Russia, among others, fell into this dark abyss and 'played god', destroying whomever they decided was unworthy, threatening or undesirable. Only when we understand that these seven universal principles are the laws of the Supreme Creator of all of life, can we understand that they can never be changed, just as the Infinite One does not change. Only when we approach them as absolute truths can we remain true to them and not dilute them with subjective or relativistic human thinking. This is another reason why the rejection of idolatry and blasphemy and all their implications are the foundations of the following five principles. The foundation of ethics and civility must be based on faith in, and attachment to, a Higher Order, an Absolute Truth.

In the course of the book these principles will be explored and expanded, both conceptually and practically, and readers will be given the tools needed to partake in this revelation as a conscious "Ben Noach" or Child of Noah. The next section will discuss the connection of the Seven Laws with the historical drama of the generation of Noah.

PRINCIPLES FOR ALL HUMANITY

Appreciating that G-d is One (no idolatry), that the Creator created all of life, and thus all of life contains a spark of Divinity, we can understand the respect and honor we need to give to the Creator (no blasphemy) and to all forms of life (no animal cruelty). This reverence behooves us to offer special compassion to human beings, who are created in the Divine image — thus, not taking life (no murder), respecting boundaries (no illicit relations), not taking from others (no theft), and actively creating a just society (establish systems of justice).

The seventh principle of justice extends to all acts of charity, social justice and civility. It includes all proper conduct between man and man, such as tending to the poor, taking care of the elderly, visiting the sick, comforting the mourners, and so on.

The more we live with the awareness of the Unity of the Creator and the fact that every single manifestation of life contains a Divine life force — from human beings created in the Divine Image, to tiny specks of dust — the more we will act with respect for the dignity of man and all of life. This is because the Oneness of the Creator and the justice and harmony of Creation are linked.

These seven principles were known to Adam and Noach, and then once again (around 1,000 years after Noach), revealed at

Mount Sinai. Indeed, ever since then, accepting the Seven Laws should not be considered merely a matter of logic or 'natural law', rather, as receiving a transmission from Mount Sinai.

As consciousness is rising in the world, and we are edging closer and closer to redemption, a time when all good people will live in harmony and peace and the world will be filled with Divine wisdom. Clearly, all those who have adhered to these seven basic principles will partake in that 'World to Come', as a consequence of their spiritual and ethical practice which made this world-wide redemption possible. All righteous people of the world, those who kept these basic principles and thereby projected righteousness and goodness to those around them, will experience eternal life and the World to Come.

HUMANITY IN A COVENANT
WITH THE CREATOR

What has been called 'monotheism', awareness of the oneness of the Creator, was not originally revealed to the world through Moshe / Moses at Mount Sinai. Rather, from the very beginning of the human experience, in the story of Adam and Chavah / Eve, and later in the story of Noach / Noah and the Great Flood, absolute monotheism was understood, felt and lived. And so were these seven basic principles of Creation. This doesn't mean that all the keepers of these principles were 'perfect'; this path is not a 'razor's edge' of perfectionism. Quite the opposite; when they fell in some way, they humbly acknowledged their mistakes, and this allowed them to spring even higher than before. They were able to rise again and turn back to the oneness and the way of life that flows from oneness — pulling all of Creation closer to redemption.

But after the time of Noach, a detour began. The arrogance of perfectionism crept in and people stopped turning back to the Creator when they fell. Coupled with the rise of many ancient civilizations, the concept of a plurality of divine forces took hold. Indeed, over time, the awareness of the Oneness of the Creator and an adherence to these fundamental principles were almost forgotten. Idolatry and mythology again spread throughout the world, along with their twisted ideas of what was socially acceptable and personally beneficial. Even horrific acts of human sacrifice and violation of marriage relationships were widely condoned and established as ritual practices. When the Torah was revealed at Mount Sinai, the Divine principles of oneness and human righteousness were reintroduced to the world, and re-established forever as objective standards of consciousness and behavior. This revelation offered a way of life that allows all human beings to reach their full potential in a conscious relationship with their Creator.

When the first human being was created and placed in the Garden of Eden, that being was embraced an idyllic state of childlike blissful innocence. At the same time, it was instructed to "work it and protect" the garden. This means man was created to reveal and cultivate the potential beauty of Creation. It is our responsibility to manifest the abundance, blessings and beauty of this "garden". The world is a Divine Garden and we are the gardeners, irrigating the garden with every thought, word and action.

As the culmination and crown of Creation, man was given the role to steward the planet and to fill the earth with wisdom and compassion. To tend to the Divine Garden effectively, man was endowed with a deep sensitivity to all of life and an ability to choose. This role was the grand plan, yet, man himself began to follow subjective interpretations of "protecting the garden", and eventually chose other plans. Gradually, human selfishness, and a destructive craving to grab and acquire things at the expense of others, became dominant in the world. Theft became a way of life, as did self-centered carnal indulgences. Distorting their gifts and actively violating the grand plan of Creation engendered the need for a radical 'reset'.

Only a physical and spiritual flood could wash away the accumulated negativity and allow a new, fresh world to emerge. This was the Great Flood of Noah. After this intensive cleansing, the new world needed to be sealed with a different kind of protectant: a covenant between the Creator and all of humanity; a sacred commitment to benefit the Creation in the way embodied by Noach himself.

Noach's reliance upon the Creator, and his rescuing every living being from the floodwaters and nurturing them in the Ark, became the essence of the new commitment of his offspring. As his family were the only ones to survive the Great Flood and inhabit the new world, all human beings are his offspring, the B'nei Noach, the "Children of Noach".

While the Seven Principles are an elaboration on the original command to "cultivate and protect the Garden," these principles formed a new "covenant" — a mutual agreement that had new objective clarity and urgency. In the wake of the traumas of the Flood, we, the Children of Noach, urgently needed the security of a promise of our survival. Therefore, we readily agreed to take responsibility for ourselves, the earth and its inhabitants, and the Creator has agreed to ensure the survival and thriving of the human family as a whole.

To live in accordance with these seven basic laws is to live in sync with the Creator's will and intention for Creation as a whole as well as each person in particular. Why might the Seven Principles of this covenant appear logical and even instinctual to us? They were ingrained in the spiritual 'DNA' of all human beings. They are the basic framework of our collective Divine mission and path, etched into our collective consciousness. This is why our happiness depends on our active practice of the Seven Principles; violating them hurts us on a deep, subconscious level and at the root of our existence.

What is the Creator's will and intention? It was "created so that it might be settled" (Yeshayahu/Isaiah, 45:18). 'Settled' here implies a level of civility and proper conduct, which is achieved by these Seven Mitzvos / commands. Our collective survival depends on civility. Therefore our responsibility as humans is, as much as we can, to ensure a settled world, a world where all humans can live in harmony, in peace with others and with nature.

We are all created in the Divine Garden and our collective task is to be the gardeners and beautifiers — to rectify the world and our body and mind, and cause them to sprout, elevate and blossom into their true spiritual and evolutionary glory. We must constantly remove the weeds of ugliness, hate, and corruption while nourishing and fertilizing the spiritual soil of the world. We must prune our self-serving drives in order to fill the garden with colorful beauty, love, and goodness, and prepare it to be a fitting place for the Infinite One to rest and dwell.

This is the purpose, and the incredible blessing, of the Seven Principles.

01

LIVING CONNECTED:
BECOMING A CO-CREATOR
OF YOUR EXISTENCE

THE FIRST OF THE SEVEN PRINCIPLES is the foundation of the other six: absolute monotheism and the negation of all forms of idolatry. Negating idolatry means moving away from worshiping any power other than the One, such as occult powers and false deities — anything with form and anything 'created'. In its modern, broad definition, this principle includes negating the 'deification' of any human being, of money, security, fleeting pleasures, power, or fame — anything apart from the Creator. We do not seek salvation or blessings from anything with a form because the True Source of Goodness is without form or limitation.

'Absolute monotheism' is a faith in the fact that there is a Single Source of Power upon which we rely for all our needs. Our life depends only upon the One Creator of All Life, acknowledging that the Creator intimately loves us and cares about what we are doing and desires that we take care of ourselves, each other and this world.

One effective way to cultivate this awareness that the Single Source of All is always with us is to carve out a time or times each day to take 'moments of silence' during which to open up and feel the presence of the Divine. This simple silence can become a contemplation and affirmation of the fact that there is "an Eye that observes all, an Ear that listens to all, and everything we do is recorded and written in a Heavenly 'book'". In other words, our Creator is always 'watching' over us, listening empathetically and compassionately 'recording' our progress, rewarding goodness, and noting where we can improve. When we realize that our Creator 'surrounds us' with guidance and support, designing all of our experiences in life for our spiritual and ethical growth, we begin to center our existence on this Singular Presence.

Again and again, we take up the commitment not to subtly worship anyone or anything other than the Creator, the One who renews the Act of Creation at every moment in infinite wisdom, giving life to the entire universe and everything in it.

Having faith in the Creator of all Life means understanding that "the nature of the Good is to give goodness." The Giver of Life is infinitely good, always seeking our best interest and finding ways to fill our lives with goodness. The Creator of life 'desires' to give life. Knowing that "Everything G-d does, He does for the best" enables us to say, in any situation in life, "This too is for the good." There is no need to seek goodness from any limited form or separate individual, for every authentic goodness in the world is a reflection of the One Giver of Goodness.

This is a fundamental principle to live by, and one that ensures peace of mind and inner joy. There is a Creator who designs this world with intention, and thus your life is not random, events are not happenstance, you are never alone in this world, and your loving Creator cares about you, and seeks your inner and outer success.

DAY TO DAY APPLICATIONS OF THIS PRINCIPLE

In the post-modern world there are various challenges that society—and therefore individuals—are contending with. In a post modernist morality vacuum there is a lack of moral clarity, and a loss of a sense of direction and purpose. The post modernist lives without a clear sense of right and wrong and devoid of a higher purpose. Without a defined sense of meaning, a person may sink into a space of anxiety and depression.

Community is another victim of postmodernism. In today's secular culture, individuals are often starved for a healthy sense of community and belonging. Owing to the lack of moral clarity, direction, and purpose, many individuals find themselves joining unhealthy, racially divisive, chauvinistic, or even harmful forms of 'religions,' or social groups, both on and offline. These groups may provide a fleeting sense of clarity, direction, and community, but ultimately, they foster division and destruction and do not offer genuine fulfillment or positive growth.

And so you ask, what is the fix for an ailing society? It is simply a life filled with connectivity to a Higher Source. This automatically brings moral clarity, a sense of purpose, and a feeling of community and belonging. Here are some examples of how living with the awareness of a Higher Force can counter these societal ailments.

1) Moral Clarity: In the confused morality of a post-moral world, there is a tendency to view weaker individuals as inherently good and more powerful people as inherently bad, regardless of their actions or the effort they put into their achievements. This has become true on an individual level and a collective level and even on a national level. The belief in Hashem provides a clear moral framework, helping individuals distinguish between right and wrong. This guidance is invaluable for making ethical decisions, navigating life's challenges with integrity and empathy, and understanding the world more clearly.

2) Sense of Purpose: With this confusion and lack of moral clarity, people have lost their sense of purpose, both individually and nationally. Faith in Hashem often gives people a sense of purpose and direction in life. It can provide a deeper understanding of one's place in the world and the reason and purpose for their country, and the meaning behind life's events, fostering a sense of fulfillment and motivation.

3) Community and Belonging: And finally, the belief in Hashem can create a strong sense of community, "one nation under G-d," providing support and companionship. This sense of belonging is crucial for emotional well-being and can prevent individuals from turning to unhealthy or harmful groups in search of clarity and connection.

01

A Deeper Perspective of Principle 01

CO-CREATORS OF OURSELVES

Part of this principle's broader implication is deep empowerment in life. It may seem to be a paradox, but when we give ourselves over to faith in our Source alone, we become 'receptors' of the greatest power of the Universe, the Creator Himself. We are vested with a Divine image, and in this way are empowered to be co-creators in our life's unfolding. We are given the ability to choose.

When man was created, the verse in Genesis says, "Let Us create man." Who is the plural 'Us'? This is the Creator talking to you and me and saying, 'Let us together create who you will become. I am going to give you the context of your life; your family, genetics, your body, and certain inclinations and proclivities, but ultimately, you will have to choose how you are going to articulate your life.'

You have choice to rise above or submit to the circumstances given to you. You are empowered to automatically react to events or to intentionally respond to them. The Creator tells us, as it were, 'I gave you the template and the empty canvas, the brushes and every kind of paint. Through your choices, we will paint together. But ultimately, what that painting becomes, is your choice.'

You are a co-creator of your experience; you can be what you want to be.

AN INEVITABLE WORLD

Let's understand this truth of empowerment a little more deeply. To our observation, every creation and form of existence emerges from another form of existence. Every action flows from a previous action, and every choice is based on previous choices. This seems to imply that our lives and the world itself are self-contained, wrapped in a rigid paradigm of cause and effect, action and reaction. If so, the possibility of genuine free choice is merely an illusion.

In a linear dimension of time, the past creates the present, and the present inevitably gives rise to the future; the choices we can make today are based on the choices we made yesterday. Yesterday's choices are shaped by prior ones, and ultimately all are rooted in our parents' choices, our ancestor's choices, our genetics and nurture. We have to ask ourselves: is free choice really possible? Can I change the course of my life? Can I choose to do good?

We all yearn for some measure of freedom from our innate predisposition, so we can feel like we are creating real choices in our lives. We may even aspire to genuine freedom or what existentialists call 'radical freedom' — in which we can truly choose without outer influences or inner reactions directing us. But is such freedom actually attainable? If we examine our lifespan, we might get the sense that our every major choice was at least heavily influenced by an outer or inner cause or condition. Perhaps we will even get the sense that the narrative of our life was predetermined, and we never actually made any choices, but were just swept along, our present experiences being no more than results of the past and predictors of the future.

True, in a created, evolving universe, once something is set into motion, the ripple effects are interminable. Every effect can be traced to a cause, and the cause in turn is merely an inevitable effect of a previous cause. Such is the nature of a self-contained system. To an observer, this may appear to be the case. However, the truth is, the only cause of everything is the Creator, Who is, by nature, absolutely free and timeless. This is not a self-contained system, rather an open, fluid, Divine contained system.

Whereas phenomena and experiences may seem to be predictive 'causes', every single phenomenon and experience in this world is actually an 'effect' of the Sole Cause. The only influencer is the Creator, and so every creation is influenced only by the Creator, and nothing else. There are not multiple causes and influences to attend to in life, like multiple deities demanding attention and service. There is only One. When we place our attention on the One Cause, when we serve our Creator, we can then have choice; we can have influence over our present and future, and even our past. We can break the chains of the 'inevitable' world.

DIVINE SPARK WITHIN: THE POWER TO CREATE

We are each gifted a 'spark' of the Infinite Light, our Creator. This 'spark' is our soul, a Divine inheritance that gives each of us the ability to become co-creators of our lives. We may not control what life places before us, such as whether it is sunny or rainy, or whether another person insults or praises us. We do have the power to choose how we are going to process and respond to such stimuli. We may not be able to control what life throws at us, but we can control what we throw back. We can choose how we are going to live our life, no matter what.

Whenever we make conscious responses and decisions, we are activating the light of our soul, the Divine gift of free will. The One Cause allows us to become the 'cause' of our life.

LIVING FROM THE OUTSIDE OR FROM THE INSIDE

We can view ourselves as a determining factor or as a predetermined outcome. This is the fundamental choice we all have to make: we can either be the 'cause' and creator of our life or we can be the 'effect' and creation of what life presents. In other words, we can live from the 'inside out', intentionally influencing and creating the painting of our life — or we can live from the 'outside in', passively being affected, formed and colored by our environment.

Each individual experiences life in two simultaneous realities, the outer world and the inner world. Broadly speaking, the outer world is what comes into us through our senses — what we see, hear, touch, taste or smell. Our inner world is how we process, think and feel about these sensations. There is what you eat; this is very important, but equally important is how you eat. Do you eat with awareness or with abandon? Do you eat to live or do you live to eat? The what determines what you put into your mouth, the how determines how you chew, digest and integrate it.

Living as if you were at the effect of life means that your external circumstances dictate your internal state of mind. This perspective implies that your inner life is solely the effect of all the outside 'causes' you encounter. Living as the 'creator' of your life means that you decide how you are going to feel and live; you become the cause of your own life, not just the effect of a random set of circumstances.

In order to simplify this idea and provide an example from day-to-day life, let's say that you wake up in the morning and it is rainy and gloomy outside. Do you automatically feel depressed? If so, you are approaching life from the outside in, as an effect rather than a cause of your reality. In this scenario, the weather is dictating how you are going to feel. The same is true if you wake up in the morning and the sun is shining and you think to yourself, "Today is going to be a great day!" Again, the outside world is dictating how you are going to feel internally. But if you wake up in the morning and you declare: "Today is going to be a great day, rain or shine," then you are choosing, and creating your day. You are thus the cause of how your day is going to be no matter what happens.

When we surrender our free will to the circumstantial sensory stimulus of the outside world then we live our life as a mere effect. However, if we live our life from the inside out, we choose how we are going to deal with what we encounter and experience. Our inner world becomes an active participant in the larger context of life.

There are people who must endure some form of personal tragedy in order for them to develop a more compassionate side of their personality. There are those who must be showered with love and acceptance in order for them to feel open and confident. Similarly, there are people that need to be smiled at in order for them to smile; they need to be complimented to feel good about themselves, and conversely, they feel down when they are criticized. These are all instances of living from the outside in. Their external circumstances dictate their lives. Place them in a beautiful, loving environment and they feel wonderful, place them in a cramped, stressful place, and they feel terrible.

People who allow circumstances to dictate their inner state tend to blame everyone and everything around them for how their life is unfolding. True, others may have wronged or hurt them, but instead of owning their feelings and choosing how to respond, they end up living as victims. Yes, there is a lot to be improved in the world, certainly, some people start life off in better circumstances than others, but our thoughts are ours. We have the ability, connected to our Creator, to live creatively, not reactively or hopelessly. Additionally, each soul needs its conditioning and challenges in order to rise and flower. Each person's experience is intricately designed and overseen by the Ultimate Designer to ensure the conditions for that individual to reach their maximum spiritual potential. Complaining and blaming does not allow this potential to unfold.

Then there are people who live from the inside out — despite their pain, they choose to be compassionate. Despite being 'rejected' by others, they choose to show friendship and generosity. Such people choose how they are going to interact with others and do not wait to first see how others will interact with them. And on account of their self-generated love and positivity, people around them tend to respond in kind.

We never really 'find' ourselves in a predicament, we place ourselves in a predicament. Usually, we either choose to be in that situation, or we 'choose not to choose' and remain in that situation, reacting with negativity and blame. But the truth is, we have a Divine-like power in the deepest part of ourselves that is 'part of the Creator', Who is the Influencer, the Source, the Cause. This means we always have the power to cease from blaming and get ourselves out of any predicament.

Always remember, "If you have the power to destroy, you also have the power to repair." If you can place yourself in a predicament, you can certainly remove yourself from it.

BEING CONNECTED WITH THE CREATOR ALLOWS US TO BE A CREATOR

The more we cultivate a living relationship with the Source of All Life, the more like the "source" we become and the more we get to live as the 'creator', the 'cause' of our lives.

We are all gifted with a spark of the infinite light of the Creator — our soul is a Divine inheritance that gives us the ability to become co-creators of our own lives, so long as we choose to live in harmony with the Truth. When we are in need, we can pray to the One Source, and when we sense fear or feel alone, we can turn to the One for comfort. Doing so activates our Divine spark and allows us to freely choose, to climb out of any predicament, and to co-create our existence, to paint the picture of our life in a most elegant way.

THE CREATOR AS GOOD

Part of cultivating a living relationship with the Source of all Life is the recognition that the Creator cares about Creation, and seeks the Ultimate goodness for Creation. As explored above, the nature of the Creator of Life is to further life and give goodness to His Creation. Indeed "Everything the Creator does is for the best," and this allows us to affirm in every situation, "This too is for the good."

As the Creator is good, life is inherently good, and we are inherently good. The Creator imbues the world with deliberate intention and nothing in it is an accident. In the same way, nothing in our life has ever been random, or an accident, or inherently negative. Our experiences and even all our choices and actions, were designed with a positive purpose, to bring us to realize goodness, hope, value and meaning. The key to our essential goodness is Teshuvah, 'conscious return' to our Source, return to free choice.

Even any acts of anger, greed, vengeance, or despondency were, and are, invitations to Teshuvah. They were, and are, wake-up calls, showing us that we were choosing not to choose. For whatever reason, we did not know that life is good and we are good. But even this was for the good, because it is never too late to return to the One Ultimate Goodness, and embrace our essential goodness, and re-focus our lives on doing good.

When we make Teshuvah, we create the possibility for others to do the same. The more we appreciate the fact that we are a creation of the Infinitely Good One, the stronger our ability is to choose a deeper and higher redemptive reality. The more we consciously embrace goodness, the more all creatures are filled with optimism, gaining momentum in the ever-increasing march toward redemption.

LIVING FEARLESS AND COURAGEOUSLY

Consciously connecting ourselves to the Source of all Goodness allows us to live with less fear. Ever since the so-called 'death of god' (the seeming triumph of secularism and scientific materialism over revelation and faith) what has emerged instead is the 'birth of death'. In other words, many people are plagued by a devastating fear of death and old age.

People are generally apprehensive about the future, but in our age, they live with more existential anxiety than ever before. When people stop believing in the One Creator, they believe in nothing, and as a result they often start believing in anything. This anything often includes all types of conspiracy theories and 'idol worship', and this in turn fosters even greater fear and more invasive anxiety.

People may intellectually accept that we 'should' be responsible in our consciousness, thought, speech and action, do what we can to make the world a better place, and even be a co-partner in Creation, yet they still live without faith and fall into chronic fear and pessimism. If their underlying subconscious belief is that everything will anyways end in disaster, then they think, 'The world will ultimately end with fire or the world will end with ice, it doesn't really matter, so why do anything?'

In our own lives, as well, the 'idol' of fear whispers, 'Nothing can be done; don't make the effort.' One fears that nothing will ever come of his initiatives, but this is really fear of his own greatness. If we believed that we really mattered and that we can make a difference in the world, it would burden us with responsibility and the necessity of leaving our comfort zone. We would sometimes rather just continue to play in the sand box.

With greatness comes responsibility, because it demands of you to be so much more, to soar so much higher, and be so much more influential. It is easier to back down and live small: 'Why think you can change the world and put so much effort into doing so. You might as well kick back and live 'humbly' and 'safely', even if it means giving up on your dreams. Greatness demands great action, great speech, great thinking. It means risking everything you have accumulated through your instinctual self-protection, including your limited identity and your belief in being a victim.

A major, recurring theme in Tanach / Torah is the directive to not fear. Indeed, living with fearless openness and vulnerability allows us to risk falling and then getting up again. This inner freedom is based on a positive belief in ourselves, which is rooted in knowing that the Creator is Good.

We are not really afraid of our smallness, rather of our greatness; we are afraid to dream big for the fear that we will be disappointed. However, if we can return to who we are for a moment, if we can reach out to the Creator in prayer, we can return to the path of co-creation. It is in our hands to make efforts to live fully, but the results are in the hands of the Creator. While we attempt to fill in the content of our narrative, the Creator of the context of life, is ultimately in charge. And the Creator wants us to live big and free, without holding onto anxiety.

The great 18th Century mystic and teacher known as the Baal Shem Tov / the Master of the Good Name lost his parents as a little boy. Yet, he grew up to become one of the most positive, life-affirming, holy and wholesome people to have walked the earth. Perhaps this remarkable self-transformation was rooted in what his father told him, right before he passed on: "Son, there is nothing to fear besides the Creator Himself!" The only thing to fear is 'disappointing' our Divine Parent by not being who He created us to be.

One student of the Baal Shem Tov, Zusha of Anipoli, once quipped, "At the end of my life, when I ascend and meet the Heavenly Judge, I will not be asked, 'Why were you not more like Moses?' Rather, I will be asked, 'Why were you not more like Zusha?'"

The Creator is Good, and we are good, and life is full of opportunities to reveal this.

TAKEAWAYS /PRACTICES

- Our first waking moments contain the potential of the entire day. Our thoughts and words upon awakening are the foundation of all our thoughts and words throughout the day. To ensure that they resonate with positivity and empowerment rather than reactivity and victimhood, we need to seize the moment and engage in a spiritual practice.

- Therefore, upon awakening, immediately thank the Creator for giving you new life. Recognize the gift of waking up and having your soul restored to your body.

- Generate feelings of gratitude and flood your mind with positivity. Choose to shine your Divine spark and act on your soul's mission in this world.

- Remember throughout the day that we can either control or allow ourselves to be controlled by our circumstances. How we respond is our choice. We may not be able to control what life throws at us, but we can control what we throw back. Therefore, practice pausing before every response to people and situations, pausing for clarity and then choosing your response.

02

ACCEPTING WHAT IS
TRANSFORMING
FRUSTRATION AND ANGER

THE SECOND PRINCIPLE, related to the first and also a foundational principle, is the directive not to curse your Creator; not to commit blasphemy. No matter how disappointed or angry you may be, do not take it out verbally against your Creator. Deeds usually follow our words, so it is important to nip negativity in the bud.

The foundation of this principle is humbly acknowledging the existence of the Creator, the Source of Life, the Cause of Everything, the Ultimate Good who wishes our goodness. Denying or rejecting the existence of the Creator, or "cursing" our Source, is to deny the source and essence of our very own life.

DAY TO DAY APPLICATIONS
OF THIS PRINCIPLE

Words matter. By us using blasphemes words towards the Creator of all Life, it may seem merely disrespectful, and of course, that is true. However, more devastatingly for our personal lives, is the fact that using such words, and sadly, many 'curse' words in various languages are in fact 'cursing of the sacred', it will affect us deeply.

Here are three ways in which blasphemy can affect us.

1) Guiding Actions: The words we choose will eventually guide our actions and behaviors. If our mouths are filled with foul language, and especially, language that is verbalized to (g-d forbid), curse G-d, curse the Source of all Life and Goodness, as in '…dam it', for example, eventually, our actions will align with those words. This can lead us to act in ways that make us feel condemned and dammed.

2) Shaping Our Emotions: Words have the power to influence our emotions. For example, affirmations and positive self-talk can boost confidence and motivation, while negative self-talk can undermine our self-esteem. If we walk around and habitually curse the Creator of all Life, we may begin to feel that life itself is cursed, and eventually and inevitably, we will feel inwardly cursed.

3) Influencing Perception: The language we use not only shapes how we feel about ourselves and the world around us but also alters our very perception of reality. Positive words, such as offering blessings instead of curses—especially refraining

from cursing the Creator—foster a positive outlook on life and oneself. Conversely, negative words lead to a more pessimistic and negative view of the world, the people around us, and ultimately, ourselves.

02

A Deeper Perspective of Principle 02
POWER OF WORDS

Words are powerful. They also open the door to thoughts, feelings and eventually, actions. Verbally blaming, denying, or belittling our Creator is the first step in potentially blocking ourselves from a healthy, loving relationship with our Creator. Once negative words are spoken, it can be more difficult for us to come back into a relationship, and this can lead to a gradual descent into a world of depravity, an absence of morals and true happiness.

Our worldview has a powerful influence over our experience. Cursing the Creator is an aspect of an idolatrous worldview. Spurning the belief in the Creator's ability to run the world leaves the person feeling that they are at the mercy of multiple clashing 'gods' or forces, unable to find real stability or lasting goodness. Without a deep belief in the One Source of Goodness, it is not possible to find contentment and happiness with one's lot, for one is always looking elsewhere, at someone else's life, or at some created object, substance or experience. Shattering one's own subtle experience of the One Divinity is the root of much frustration in life.

The more content we are with what we have, the more inner peace we have. At the same time, living without desire would leave a person lifeless, with no drive to grow and flourish. We do need to embrace our instinct to strive, yearn, push ourselves to achieve, and always aspire for more. Yet, if we approach life from an inner core of contentment, we can strive, yet know that if it is not meant that we attain or obtain something in particular, perhaps it is not meant to be. We can be content and at peace because, again, we know that making efforts is in our hands but results are in the Divine hands alone.

'Blasphemy' enters our consciousness when we live with persistent discontent, and can no longer find our core of inner peace and presence. Our desires then are rooted in a sense of lack. When these yearnings are not fulfilled, or when the results of our efforts are different than expected, there is anger, lashing out at others, and ultimately, lashing out at the Creator of our life.

NOT BEING ANGRY AT LIFE

In the previous chapter we discussed living with the awareness of the Source of existence, and that we are gifted with the Divine image, which is essential for a healthy, happy and productive, meaningful existence. We also explored how we are invited to live without fear, rather with hope and positivity, and this nurtures our innate ability to choose how we will respond to circumstances. We can choose to respond to life without jealousy or anger.

NOT 'WHY?' RATHER, 'FOR WHAT PURPOSE?'

Whatever has happened was supposed to happen. All you can do is learn to respond with openness and clarity, not be reactive and feed fear and anger. Instead of living your life with the demand, 'Why did this happen to me,' live with the question, 'What is the ultimate purpose of this experience?'

When we ask 'why', we are stuck in a mental focus on the past, searching for answers that can never satisfy us. Instead of trying to trace the 'genealogy' and history of an unpleasant experience, whose fault it is, or how we failed in some way, we can place our focus on the hidden future benefit. In this way, we can resist the illusion of false certainty which is the same illusion at the basis of 'mythology': the false sense of knowing why things happen. Thinking we know — or need to know — why things happen, focusses our mind on pinpointing independent causes and judging them. But when we shift our attention instead toward the deeper purpose in what happened, we remain fully present in the moment, and open to the redemptive future.

In truth, we can never really know why things happen in the wider sense, since only the Creator knows every side of every story. But we can make a choice regarding what we will do with our story.

When we ask 'why,' we are looking to avoid responsibility, placing it on external forces, and subtly implying that the Creator is not aware of and in charge of everything. When we ask 'toward what end', we are claiming responsibility for the co-creation of the new now, while acknowledging that the Creator has a greater plan.

Whether we remain stuck in predictable repetition, or choose to listen and learn to create a better future for ourselves, depends on our ability to ask ourselves, "What could I possibly learn from this situation?" To trust that whatever happens, happens for the sake of growth and redemption helps us extract abundant meaning and motivation. We can let go of anger and disappointment and move forward into the ever-new future.

CHOOSING OUR RESPONSES

Underlying acts of angry reactivity is an 'ideology' of idolatry. In reacting angrily, we are declaring: I reject what the Creator is manifesting here. I know better than Him, and I have a more accurate idea of how things should be.

Of course, if a person just cut you off on the road, he may have done so of his own volition and choice. And from the perspective of the present moment, events did not necessarily have to occur as they did. Knowing this is fine, but it leaves the door open for you to become angry that events did not unfold differently in the moment. And once you step through the door of anger, it closes behind you, blocking you from receiving the lesson or opportunity for personal growth offered to you by means of this event. This is because externally directed anger overwhelms your ability to be self-reflective.

When something that has already happened, it is actually most helpful to see it as essentially 'meant to be'. We should therefore try to accept the fact that for some perhaps unknown reason we needed this experience in order to learn or do something positive. By instead rejecting it and becoming angry, we are effectively saying: My reality was tampered with by this other person. This was not meant to be; the Creator has nothing to do with this. I have no Divine protection, so I must rely on myself and launch a counter-attack.

We always have the choice to make healthy, productive, life-affirming responses. And we always have the opportunity to simply begin again when we fall off the path. As human beings made in the Divine Image, choosing our responses is our greatest blessing and our greatest responsibility.

IF ONLY IS HERESY

A subtle posture of anger at life or at oneself is the 'if only' mentality. One complains, 'If only I did this or that,' 'If only I was there and not here,' 'If only I was born rich,' 'If only I had been raised another way,' 'If only my parents cared,' 'If only the boss would notice my good work,' or 'If only I had not made that fateful mistake.' Say the sages of absolute Monotheism, this is essentially heresy. The past is done and was meant to be — because the Creator, in His inscrutable wisdom, is designing creating all events in time, and is doing so for the ultimate good.

LETTING GO OF ANGER

It is not always easy for a person who has been abused to let go of anger. Our failed societal system tells them, "Your anger is bad," and this can drive the anger within or increase reactive behavior. It is vital to understand that angry emotions are designed by the All Wise Creator for a wise purpose, and they can be embraced and felt without fueling destructive actions. Acting out of anger or fury may seem to release or dissipate the feeling, but in the long term, it only exacerbates the issue and increases anger, so acting out cannot be the purpose of anger. Acting out anger is likened to handling fire, acts of retribution can physically and spiritually burn us.

Harboring thoughts of anger can harm the eyes: says Iyov / Job (17:7): "My eyes have grown dim because of anger." It clouds our higher vision and obscures our in-sight. Modern science suggests that habitually angry people develop lesions in their brains. However, when we let go of angry thinking and cease harboring them, it is possible to heal our brains, our eyes, hearts and souls, and to come into a healthier relationship with difficult emotions.

Teshuvah, turning toward the Creator, includes feeling the emotions and sensations of anger and helplessness, letting the body tremble, even maybe even 'punching a pillow', or screaming for help in prayer. In this way, Teshuvah trains us to experience this intense heat and energy without acting them out and harming ourselves, others, or objects, and ultimately to humbly surrender our anger to the Creator.

While there is also a concept of holy, noble anger, the distinction between this and destructive, ego-based anger is very subtle and can be barely distinguishable. Unfortunately, unholy anger is by far the more common. Righteous anger can be calm or organized, even while intensely resolute, and it fuels only positive, compassionate action. Negative anger is not compassionate, but is impulsive, chaotic, vindictive and it causes hurt. In unholy anger, our inner eye is hidden, and all we can see is our angry, self-oriented, egoic perception of reality. This is why someone who is angry is at that moment likened to an idolator.

Again, to let go of anger, one needs first to feel it and let the energy be there, yet without acting on it in destructive ways. For example, if you feel anger towards someone who hurt you, write them a letter, letting them know how you feel — but do not send the letter, rather tear it up. The mere act of writing will help you feel and release built-up tension, and bring you closer to surrendering your anger into the hands of the All-Loving Creator.

LETTING GO OF CURSING

Common cursing and foul language can lead to cursing the Creator, G-d forbid. Negative words drag us down, clog our consciousness, and create deeper reactivity. Also, every creature is connected with its Creator, so we should be careful not to denigrate any person.

Once, a scholar who was experiencing pride encountered a man with a disfigured face walking on the road and remarked, "What an ugly person! Is everyone from your city as ugly as you?" "I don't know," replied the man, "but why don't you go to the Craftsman who made me and tell Him what an ugly product He made." When the scholar realized that he had sinned and insulted this man on account of his appearance, he descended from his donkey and prostrated himself before him, and he said: "I have sinned against you; forgive me!" The man replied: "I will not forgive you until you go to the Craftsman Who made me and say: How ugly is the product you made."

Every person is made in the Image of the Craftsman, and calls for respectful speech. It is not that we need to excuse bad behavior, and it can even be positive to criticize idolatry, but the person itself is a work of the Creator, the Artist who fashions us all. In the path of the Seven Principles, it is therefore very important to begin watching your speech, and replacing negative or foul expressions with mindful, respectful ones. For example, if you have a habit of saying, "I hate this…," try saying instead, "I admit, I am having a hard time with this…." Pray to the All-Attentive Creator for help when your tolerances are low.

TAKEAWAYS / PRACTICE

- Write letters addressed to people who have stimulated your anger. Write everything you wish to express to the other person, but do not send the letters, rather tear them up.

- In general, whatever happened to you in the past was meant to happen. Perhaps it was meant to be in order that you would overcome it and help others in similar situations, or perhaps it was meant to wake you up. Realizing this will help you stop obsessing or giving the past events too much attention. To the best of our ability, we should learn from the past, and then move forward.

- Remember that simply holding onto anger is more harmful and has more power over us than the offense itself. Forgiveness is the way to release our involvement with the offender and the offense.

03

ACKNOWLEDGING THE DIVINE WITHIN OTHERS

SECURING AN AWARENESS OF THE CREATOR, sustainer of all life, brings us to the third principle: the sacredness of life.

"Anyone that sheds the blood of man will have his blood shed by man, for in His Image did G-d make man" (Bereishis / Genesis, 9:6). Every human being is created in the Divine Image, and taking a life is a desecration of this image; a desecration of the Creator Himself, as it were.

Every human life is sacred, no matter how old or young, from a feeble elder to a fetus. Each life is infinitely valuable and indispensable. The value of human life cannot be measured or quantified; even one moment of human life is infinitely precious. To help prolong someone's life, even for a moment, has unimaginable value.

DAY TO DAY APPLICATIONS OF THIS PRINCIPLE

We may own the objects in our lives, but we do not own our lives itself. Life is a sacred loan that is given to us from the Creator of Life. We are not the arbitrates to decide what life is worth or not worth living. All life is infinitely valuable and utterly indispensable, certainly it is not for us to decide who gets to live and who can be terminated, even for our own selves.

Here are three ways this principle influences our lives and the decisions we make.

1) Abortion: The moment a fetus is conceived, possibly 72 hours after the moment of intimacy, the fetus takes the status of life, to some extent, the fetus is considered a living being, albeit not yet an individual person. And therefore, under normal circumstances, such as consensual relationship, it is forbidden to terminate the life of an unborn child, and it may be akin to murder. (Although, this depends on the stage of pregnancy, within 72 hours, within forty days, and so forth). It also must be pointed out, that if the mother's life is literally endangered by the pregnancy, and the child has not yet emerged from

the birth canal, her life takes precedence over the fetus's life. (Emotional and psychological suffering, i.e.: danger, may also be taking into consideration, but it is beyond the scope of this text to delve into this highly sensitive issue).

2) Assisted Suicide: Just as we do not have the right to terminate a fetus's life at the beginning of life, we cannot end life at its conclusion—neither someone else's nor our own. Life is a loan given to us, but we do not own our lives. Yet, this does not mean that if a person is suffering, we must prolong their life with every medical experiment. In fact, we may even pray for a more immediate demise, but we are not permitted to actively terminate life.

3) Promoting Non-Violence Resolutions: Overall, this principle of the sacredness of life encourages us to resolve conflicts peacefully and certainly to avoid physical harm to others. It fosters a culture of non-violence in our interactions, whether at home, work, or in the community and the world at large.

03

A Deeper Perspective of Principle 03
WE DO NOT OWN OUR BODIES

Not taking a life includes not extinguishing one's own life. We do not ultimately own our bodies, rather they are given to us 'on loan' by the Creator for the duration of our journey on earth. Thus, we do not even have the 'right' to inflict pain upon ourselves or others. We need to honor each and every human being for their infinite value, and by extension, ensure that their needs for survival are in place. "Anyone who saves a life is as if he saved an entire world." Every human being is an entire world. As the Creator is Infinite the value of His creations is also in a sense infinite.

The directive to support life applies even when we do not see purpose in someone's continued survival; say a very sick person connected to life support machines, or, G-d forbid, an infant who was born incapable of remaining alive. From what we might call an 'influential person', to one who is severely developmentally disabled, each life is uniquely indispensable.

Imagine you are put in this very difficult ethical predicament. You are a conductor of a train. The train has just derailed and is heading to hit three young, healthy people on the tracks, but if you pull a certain lever, the train will swing to the right, away from the three people and instead hit a single person who is severely disabled and also terminally ill. The wisdom of these Seven Principles directs you in this situation not to pull that lever. You have no right to decide to let one person die in order to save three, regardless of your idea of who is more worthy of life.

The third principle calls us to cultivate a state of consciousness in which we will always honor and cherish the dignity of each person, and the Divine Image within them.

DIVINE IMAGE WITHIN SELF AND OTHERS

Speaking of the creation of mankind, the Torah says, "G-d created man in His image, in the image of G-d He created him; male and female He created them" (Bereishis / Genesis, 1: 27).

This verse is teaching us that we are created in the Divine image. Telling us. as individuals, to have self-respect, recognize our own value and greatness. It teaches us, the human beings greatness and power. A few chapters later, the verse says, "Anyone that sheds the blood of man will have his blood shed by man, for in His Image did G-d make man" (Ibid, 9:6). This teaches us about the moral limits of such power. We have power, but every human being is created in the Divine Image, and therefore we cannot use our power to deprive another person of his power or life.

The most exaggerated expression of this idea is to refrain from murder: "Anyone who sheds the blood of a person will have his blood shed by another person, for in His Image did G-d make human beings." The blood of your fellow is as red as yours.

We have power, but we need to use it wisely and with compassion. certainly not to, Heaven forbid, use that power to murder or innovate more creative ways to harm or kill another.

Of course, self-defense is not an issue of "murder"; both individuals and nations are allowed to defend themselves: "If someone stands up to kill you, you may kill him (first)." We cannot be naive, yet we need a lot of sensitivity and wisdom to know when and how to defend ourselves, to know who is an actual mortal enemy, and to know when we are actually under lethal threat. If the permission to kill in self-defense is misused, it is indeed "murder".

POWER VERSUS FORCE

We have power, in fact infinite power, being created in the Image of the All Powerful One. And we can and should wield this power for good. It is vital that 'power' is not to be confused with 'force'. True power is not power over others, rather for others.

People tend to use the words 'power' and 'force' interchangeably. Here, 'power' refers to an effect of a deeper alignment with the Supreme Power of the universe. A truly powerful person is powerful due to the fact that they emulate and become conduits of the Supreme Power. Just as the Creator tolerates and supports all, a person becomes powerful by tolerating and supporting the abundant diversity of Creation, helping others and lifting them up.

Conversely, the use of 'force', brutality or violence, or Heaven Forbid, stooping to the level of murder, is a symptom of powerlessness. Those who demand to be served, obeyed or esteemed, usually have the lowest self-esteem. A powerless individual feels the need to control and force others, in an attempt to mask their fear of loss of control or sense of powerlessness.

To use the great power of our Divine Image, the image of the Giver of Life, we must give life, and not end life. We need to assist others and not take from them; we need to serve others and not selfishly deny their rights or wellbeing. Only then can we authentically feel empowered. Recognizing the Divine image within ourselves is synonymous with recognizing the Divine image within others. True power is not threatened, rather it celebrates the other for their own unique expression of the Divine Image, and reveres the One Who is refracted into the diversity of His Creation.

TRUE PEACE IS THE INCLUSION OF DIVERSITY

Recognizing the Divine Image (in Hebrew, *Tzelem Elokim*) within others allows us to honor and celebrate their uniqueness and 'otherness'. If we are fully engaged, alive and conscious of the Ultimate Power of the universe, we will by nature "receive all men with a pleasant countenance," and "receive every person with joy."

Even when we see something within another not to our liking, and even if we are right to have such an opinion, yet, we should see if we can judge them favorably. Just as disrespecting others is essentially disrespecting the honor of their Creator, so viewing others favorably is essentially viewing the Creator favorably.

To consciously and creatively always find the merit in another person's actions. Most people act out, not because they are bad people per se, but rather, because they are missing something in their lives, love, respect, self-worth. While we still need to defend ourselves in some way if in fact the other person is dangerous, we can still judge them favorably. It is essentially an act of love not to let another person harm you or someone else.

A child misbehaving in class or in the home is simply crying out for attention, for help. The way to help them is to try to find the points of goodness within them, nurture them, and allow them to flower and flourish. Similarly, with virtually anyone, seeing their inner goodness helps them reveal that goodness outwardly. Locating the Divine Image within another, and amplifying it, helps them reclaim it. This is because everyone wants to live with a sense of acceptance and openness, with less fear and anxiety; when someone is seen for who they really are, they usually relax and respond kindly.

Sadly, many people walk through life with a me-or-you attitude; everyone they meet is a potential threat or enemy. Most times, they are just broken and reaching out. If safe and possible, we can offer them a virtual spiritual embrace by seeing their inner 'point of goodness' within, allowing that to come to the surface.

To bring the world toward redemption, we need to find our shared humanity, locating and revealing the Divine Image in everyone around us. The deepest soul of each person is revealed differently, and that is what makes this world such a beautiful tapestry. The Creator created everyone in a distinct way. Shalom / peace is not the elimination of distinctions and differences, rather it is the integration of diverse parts into a whole.

NOT 'KILLING' OTHERS EMOTIONALLY

A broader, subtler implication of this principle is not embarrassing others, for embarrassing a person is likened to killing them. Shaming others is a type of psychological murder as it steals their sense of aliveness, their confidence, self-worth or their goals and ambitions.

For instance, if a child or any impressionable person were to speak in public, and someone in the audience smirked, or made a face, that could be the last time the person had the strength to speak in public. If someone came to you excited about a new idea or plan they wished to undertake, and you simply dismissed them, you could be 'killing' them spiritually or emotionally, robbing them of their dreams or their future.

If a young child says, 'I want to be the richest person in the world,' or 'I want to grow up to be the greatest sage of the generation,' allow them this dream. Never mock them; life itself is challenging enough. Be there to listen, to offer encouragement, to give them power, to allow them to explore their ideas safely. Cultivate, sustain and nourish their creativity, their inner image of the Creator. In this way we access our own Divine qualities, as well as allow others to do the same.

TO BE A CREATOR IS TO MANIFEST LOVE

The opposite of 'killing' or harming is loving, and so the fullness of the principle of 'no killing' is lovingkindness and benefiting others. Now, switching from a lifestyle of even subtle harm to a lifestyle of lovingkindness sounds very difficult. It is therefore extremely helpful to realize that the foundation of Creation is Divine love — the act of Creation itself was an act of lovingkindness. "The world is founded on (Divine) kindness / giving" (Tehilim / Psalms,

89:3). It was in order to reach out to an 'other' and give it goodness, that the Creator fashioned a world. Thus, love is the very fabric of Creation and our lives.

Love is also the one 'attribute' or quality that we can, with logical certainty, ascribe to the Creator. As we, who are created in the Divine Image, contain a trace of the 'Creator' within our soul, creative acts of love are also innate in us. This is seen in our Divine instinct to procreate, and also our deep drive to further and advance Creation through ideas and technologies, and to benefit mankind and the entire world through every means possible. This is the way we manifest our Divine Image; the more lovingkindness we express and enact, the more Divine-like we are.

LOVE EXTENDS OUTWARDS

Our Creator, created us through unconditional love in order to empower us to love unconditionally, as well.

Love starts with loving yourself. This does not mean 'being in love with yourself', which is mere narcissism — rather, truly loving yourself is seeing the good in yourself and benefiting yourself, your soul and your body. We should not rob ourselves of aliveness by beating ourselves up, adopting an ill perception of ourselves, or constantly knocking ourselves down. Just as we need to listen to and encourage a child, we need to compassionately listen to ourselves and encourage ourselves; to nurture our aspirations to grow and be more, to 'give life' to who we really are.

We need to judge ourselves favorably, and to cultivate a healthy sense of self-respect and inner security in ourselves. And we need to love ourselves so that we can begin to extend the circle of love to those around us. "Love your neighbor as yourself:" once we have love and respect for ourselves, we can extend authentic love to others beginning with those closest to us.

Often, it seems easier to love a total stranger than to love your parents or in-laws, for example. It is also possible to feel more love for people who share your values and mindset, than the people in your life who, in a sense, deserve your love the most. Sometimes people even feel more love for their pets, their gardens, than other human beings. But real love, by nature, embraces your family and the people in your community before it widens to include strangers and all human beings — and only then does it include members of the animal, vegetable and mineral kingdoms. Like water, love first fills the self before it overflows upon the people closest to us; then it spreads out to cover wider groups of people and general populations before it covers species that are more and more 'distant' from us, and finally impersonal phenomena as well.

Love is the very foundation of our existence, but, sadly, many people are not in touch with it. This is why someone can seem to skip over loving people and show more love to animals or cars, and so forth. Sadly, such love can bring with it cruelty to humans, as if their love for people has been spent on their pet or their car, leaving their reserves of love empty. A blanket declaration such as 'I love everyone,' is meaningless, unless you can first love this particular person and that particular person, in widening circles until your love has authentically expanded to include 'everyone'.

LIFE IN THE PRESENT:
LIVING HEAVEN OR A LIVING HELL

With deliberate practice we will be able to expand our embrace of the Creator's beautiful world, and with sensitivity and without naivete, to see the goodness or Divine image within others. When we can see the goodness within someone even when it is deeply hidden, when we have the acumen and dexterity to unearth those deeper inner recesses of the person's soul, we become able to see Divine goodness everywhere, even to the point at which life becomes blissful and heavenly.

When we are able to walk this earth with eyes wide open, with wonderment, relaxed excitement, and effortless elation, delighting in the goodness of Creation — this is a subjective experience of 'heaven on earth'. We are both transcending negativity and embracing everything in our experience.

In such a heavenly state of mind, there is the maturity to realize that our enjoyment does not come at the expense of another person. Happiness is not taken from someone else, and wellbeing is not 'purchased' by causing oneself or others to suffer. There is never a need to 'eliminate' another person or silence them in order for us to be happy or at peace. Happiness and peace are everywhere because the Divine Presence is everywhere.

Unfortunately, many people still experience this earthly realm as if it is a living nightmare, a living hell. A hell state is where every person one meets is suspected of being an enemy, and every experience one has is frustrating or potentially threatening. Hell is to be in a state of total conflict with oneself, with others, with the world as a whole, or with the Creator. Heaven, on the other hand, is to be in harmony with others, with oneself, with the world and with the Creator.

Long ago, in a small, poor village in Poland, there lived a wealthy and pious man by the name of Isaac. One day, Isaac invited all the leaders of the community to an evening banquet, promising them a feast worthy of Gan Eden / Paradise. Upon their arrival, each of the guests was escorted to the table and to their very own place setting. As soon as Isaac entered the room, he sat down and summoned the butler, who came and placed before him a bowl of delicious hot soup. Oddly enough, soup was not offered to any of the other guests. Sipping his soup Isaac exclaimed, "Oh, what a delicious soup! I am sure, my friends, that you have never tasted such a tasty soup."

After the soup the next course was brought in, and once again the guests weren't served. Again, Isaac exclaimed how delicious the food was. Losing patience, one of the guests blurted out: "Isaac, have you invited us to make a mockery out of us? You promised a feast worthy of Paradise, and here, not only did we not get to eat but we have to suffer watching you eat."

Isaac smiled. "Indeed, this meal is worthy of Paradise! "You see," he said, "Paradise is a state of mind in which people love each other enough that they can take pleasure in another person's happiness. There is no envy or jealousy in Paradise, only love and understanding. And now that you have understood this, dinner will be served."

Heaven is inclusive and hell is exclusive. In a heavenly state, there is me and you, in hell there is me or you. Whether we live with the blissful feeling of heaven or the agonizing dread of hell is based on the choices we make. Throughout this life we can choose to be in heaven by including others, or in hell by eliminating, judging or excluding others. And of course, the way we live in this world affects the way we experience the next world.

We are faced with an ongoing choice. Will we use our innate G-dly qualities of our Divine Image to further life, to empower ourselves and others, to create benefit, innovation and beauty, and to seek the welfare of all human beings? Or will we live closed off and shout down, seeing everyone and everything as a threat or a potential loss? We can take the higher road or the lower road; a path of happiness and 'giving life', or a path fraught with tension, anxiety and 'taking life' from others.

TAKEAWAYS /PRACTICES

- Cultivate respect and even love for others. Begin by thinking about the things you love about yourself, your strong points. Now, recognize the positive and good qualities within someone close to you. Maybe they are messy, for example, and that triggers tension and judgmentalism in you, yet in that 'messiness', they are also more spontaneous and freer. Focus on that freedom.

- Take a few minutes today for the following visualization, designed to help you expand your 'circle' of love. Close your eyes and visualize yourself walking into a room where one of the most beloved persons in your life — perhaps your spouse or child — is sleeping peacefully. Open your heart to feel the tremendous love and acceptance you have for that person, and also their love for you. There is no judgment or tension, just love. After resting in this feeling for a short time, imagine more people whom you also love, walking into the room; feel your love flowing toward them as well. Slowly, allow more people into the room, those with whom you are not so close but still friendly, and expand your feelings of warmth toward them. Then welcome in someone for whom you feel unresolved tension, and allow your love and acceptance extend to them as well. Continue, in this way, enlarging your circle of acceptance and love.

- Remember, every encounter with another is an opportunity for growth. Everyone has something to teach you. A wise person learns from everybody. Contemplate what you can learn from a 'difficult person' in your life, and note your insights in your Seven Principles journal.

04

LOVE WITH
BOUNDARIES & RESPECT

LIVING WITH THE PREVIOUS PRINCIPLE ensures that we use our Divine Image in a healthy, productive way, and to avoid harming or even belittling another person. Taking life or decreasing the quality of life of another destroys the unity between people and between people and the Creator. The fourth principle builds on that principle. We need to harness the libido — the drive to give life — in a way that creates unity between people and between people and Divinity. This principle guides us in how to help create healthy, productive relationships and families.

Examples of actions that grossly abuse the drive to create life, and destroy relationships and inner wellbeing, include adultery, incest, sodomy and bestiality. These types of activity must be completely avoided in order to ensure the sanctity of physical intimacy, family life, marriage, and a safe and redemptive world.

DAY TO DAY APPLICATIONS OF THIS PRINCIPLE

To greatest way to ensure that our children and the next generation are raised with a healthy sense self, well balanced and adjusted, is for them to be raised by loving parents in a family structure where there is both a father and mother and is thus properly balanced and holy. The sanctity of family life and a healthy marriage provides children with a safe environment, and gives them the sense of security and sense of belongings that is so desperately needed in today's chaotic world.

1) Commit to Marriage: Beyond physical, mental, and emotional attraction, marriage elevates us into a sacred and sanctified space. When approached with the right intentions, it allows couples to bond deeply and meaningfully, creating a Divine space of unity and holiness. However, this is a choice we must make. We need to be committed to entering such a sacred unity and dedicated to nurturing this profound connection.

2) Commit to Intimacy: Intimacy gives us a sense of wholeness, which is why we all crave it. Yet, sadly, many people in committed relationships still feel devastatingly alone. It is not enough to live under the same roof or share bank accounts

to have an intimate relationship. True intimacy requires a commitment to being open and vulnerable with each other. It goes beyond love and feelings towards each other; it involves sharing your deepest emotions, fears, and thoughts in a created space, that you both create, that is safe, secure, and non-judgmental.

3) Commit to be Committed: In a throwaway culture, where everything is disposable, from the cups we drink from to the abundance of choices available, people often sadly bring this mindset into their marriages. They do not always consider that marriage is a long-term commitment. As a result, at the first sign of not "feeling it," they may be quick to look elsewhere and give up. A fundamental requirement for any marriage to succeed is a commitment to being committed. When you take the sacredness and sanctity of marriage seriously, even if there are no children yet, you are more likely to stay dedicated. This dedication increases the potential for creating something truly beautiful, lasting, and intimate.

04

A Deeper Perspective of Principle 04

CHILDREN RAISED IN A SAFE SPACE & LOVING ENVIRONMENT

Children raised in a safe, loving home have an easier time being loving to others. As they grow older, they feel happier, more secure, self-confident and empowered to contribute to their community and society. They usually have less stress, addictions, risky behaviors or dysphoria.

Following the verse, "Anyone who sheds the blood of a person will have his blood shed by a person, for in His Image did G-d make man" (Bereishis / Genesis, 9:6), the verse continues: "Be fertile, then, and increase; abound on the earth and increase on it" (ibid, 7). The principle of not taking life or harming others dovetails into the principle of creating life and uniting with others in truly beneficial ways.

To create new life is a natural human instinct, which is designed to take people beyond focusing on self-preservation alone, and moving them toward perpetuating and benefitting our species. When this instinct is aligned with the soul, it creates deeper unity between people, allowing two individuals to become one. Harnessing the healthy libido within the confines of a committed, faithful and loving relationship allows for a highly refined form of unity. This is the deeper reason for this principle, besides the obvious repugnance of deviant or misdirected behaviors.

Once, in an attempt to rid the world of sin once and for all, the ancient sages meditatively trapped and imprisoned the libido, the eros of the entire world. Yet, the next morning, they had to release it, because "one could not find even a fresh egg in the marketplace."

Libido is the fountain of life, and so nothing is more holy than intimacy. Without a healthy drive and instinct for survival and perpetuation, everything creative, in all of Creation, comes to a standstill.

Desire is the engine that moves Creation. An acute sense of deficiency and unrealized unity drives human beings to transcend and actualize themselves, and to bring real change to the world. New scientific developments and insights into human existence are born through a sense of lack, imperfection, and a craving for more from life, yet these primal emotions must be balanced with a deeper sense of wholeness and fulfillment. When desire is not grounded in deeper wholeness, when it is unchecked and imbalanced, it becomes overwhelming, leading to obsession, jealousy, darkness and violence. When abused, nothing can be more debasing and destructive to the human being than desire.

MARRIAGE: THE OTHERNESS OF THE OTHER IS THEIR ATTRACTIVENESS

Just as this dual dynamic, yearning and desire, coupled with a deeper sense of unity and wholeness, is the meta-structure of the universe, driving it continuously toward realizing higher states of unity, it is also the setting of a healthy marriage. Two separate individuals of different genetics and upbringings desire to live together in a holy commitment as one. Two become a unified entity: "Therefore, a man leaves his father and mother and clings to his wife, so that they become one flesh" (Bereishis / Genesis, 2:24). With a lot of blessings, hopefully from the "two", will come a "one" — a child.

Two-ness or 'otherness' is actually a precondition for unification and a revelation of a greater wholeness. The longing for another is precisely a sense of otherness; we intuit that what we lack in ourselves, the other will complete. While there is a part of us that is always already complete, namely our soul, our Divine Image, which is part of the Divine Oneness, there is another part of us that is part of the world, and thus always 'incomplete'.

Relationships allow us, the incomplete self, to realize a state of completion. Yet it is also due to our differences that challenging issues arise, such as one spouse wanting to arrange their shared life in a particular way, while the other spouse wants it a different way. Sadly, what was originally charming about the other can start to become annoying.

If you think more deeply about this, you may see that the so-called 'fault' that you find in your spouse, or what you do not like about them, is directly related to their greatness. It is directly related to what you truly like about them; it is a central element of your attraction to them.

For instance, say these traits of your spouse annoy you: he or she 1) is disorganized, and 2) tends to do things impulsively, without thinking. Now, think about the traits you love about your spouse. Perhaps they are really the same traits: he or she 1) is spontaneous or a free-thinker, and 2) is always ready to get things done without hesitation.

Perhaps you judge your partner in life to be slow-to-move and rigid. Yet, upon inspection, you may very much love their steadfastness and the way they help you stay focused. This idea also applies to relationships with all kinds of people: from co-workers and bosses, to friends and relatives. What you have a hard time with is a reflection of what you enjoy about them.

Often, people are attracted to a spouse who seems to offer something like the kind of parenting they needed as a child. For example, a man whose mother was not emotionally warm, and never hugged him as a child, may seek a woman in his mother's image, who will act in similar ways. This is the subconscious mind of the man recreating the same situation, in an attempt to heal the subtle woundings he experienced as a child. Similarly, people who marry the image of an abusive parent, are subconsciously seeking a Tikun / healing or rectification of their soul and life-story.

However, it is important to understand that our Tikun in marriage is not merely to re-live our past, but it is actually to bring healing to our spouse. Say a woman is married to a man whose mother never listened to him when he spoke. If she can realize that she has similar patterns and never listens to her husband, she can activate her soul's Tikun by working on herself and listening to her spouse. In other words, your soul-Tikun is not about finding in a spouse the parent that you were missing as a child, rather it is to go against your habits and offer to your spouse what they were missing. Trying to make your spouse complete you is counterproductive. The truth is, you are in that specific relationship not to seek your own healing, but to actively offer healing to your spouse. A pair of life partners are actually one soul — healing, elevating and completing itself through 'unilateral' and even 'unrequited' giving.

MASCULINE & FEMININE COSMIC & MICROCOSMIC DYNAMIC

Marriage is a sacred space where our personal Tikkun / soul-elevation and self-actualization takes place. Is also a laboratory in which the cosmic creative process is enacted.

We all have an ability to reenact the cosmic 'creative process'. In the act of creation, the Creator, Who is metaphorically reflected in a 'masculine' quality of outward expression, creates and nurtures the universe, metaphorically reflected in a 'feminine' quality of receptivity. A healthy, balanced, respectful, loving, faithful union between masculine and feminine human beings mirrors the unity between the 'masculine' Creator and the feminine Creation. Any violation of this sacred human relationship has a ripple effect throughout the cosmos; any 'microcosmic' shattering of unity, and creates a disruption of the unity between the Creator and Creation. In a sense, it is as if the Unity of the Creator Himself is disturbed.

Peace in the home creates peace throughout all worlds. Shalom / Peace is a name of G-d. Out of respect and devotion to certain Divine Names, we avoid erasing their written forms. However, the ancient sages teach that G-d allows His name to be erased if doing so will bring peace between spouses. This is because peace, wholeness and unity in the home preserves the wholeness and unity of the Divine Name itself.

On a more 'mundane' level, the harmonious functioning and health of family units is the foundation of all ethical human societies. We need to build homes, not prisons, for our families. We need to unite families, not break them apart. There are challenges and difficulties involved, however 'family' is the training center for all interpersonal ethical behavior.

The home is the place where children learn what it means to hold fast to commitment, mutual respect, sharing, loyalty, friendship, and healthy boundaries. It is a place of giving and receiving, and a space where love and a sense of belonging flowers, and it is also where one learns how to be an individual within a relationship. No one can truly claim 'This is my husband,' or '...my wife," as no one can own someone else. We ultimately don't even own ourselves — everything and everyone belongs to the Creator alone. Nor do we own our children, though we call them 'our' children. Children come through us, not from us. They are made in the Divine's Image, not our image.

Creating wholeness in our relationships — focusing our desires upon our marriage partner, and refraining from all inappropriate or degrading relationships — brings peace and sanctity not only to our own lives and family, but to the entire spiritual cosmos. We have the power to bring the Divine Presence of Shalom into the world and never let it be 'erased'.

TAKEAWAYS / PRACTICES

- On a lower level, love is an act of exclusion: I love 'A' and thus I hate 'B'; I like this group of people, and therefore dislike the other group. On a higher rung, love is a flow that emanates from the Source of All Sources, and it is thus all-encompassingly inclusive: I love this person and thus I love all people. Ask yourself if your love is of the higher rung.

- Love follows giving; the more you give to someone, the deeper your love and investment in them will become. If you are struggling to feel love for someone, try giving to them. Similarly, if you feel a lack of love from your spouse or a friend, invite them to give to you. The act of giving fosters love, and the more they give, the more their love for you will flower.

- Remember that what you think of as another person's 'fault' is usually where their strong point lies and what you actually like about them. In your Seven Principles Notebook, list three things that annoy you about someone close to you. Now, think about three things you like about them. See if these areas are linked. If so, shift your perception to their good points and what you like.

- In your Seven Principles Notebook note any 'wounding' that your spouse may have suffered in their relationship to a parent. Consider what would be a 'corrective experience' for them; an opposite of the negative dynamic which could give them a sense of healing and wellbeing. Acting on this may be part of the Tikun / soul-elevation. After giving them this gift, note any effects on them and on yourself.

- Pray to the Creator — Shalom, the Source and Essence of Peace, for integrity in your primary relationships and in your procreative drive. Pray that you will increase peace in the world.

05

A HEALTHY RELATIONSHIP TO OWNING & POSSESSING

JUST AS WE NEED TO RELATE TO PEOPLE in a healthy and mutual manner, without a sense of ownership or obsession, we need to relate with clarity to the objects in our lives.

On a literal level, the fifth principle and directive is not to steal, and this includes overcharging a customer or client, refuting a claim of money that is owed, and actively coveting what is not yours. Even using another person's property without their permission can be considered stealing on a more subtle level.

To be aligned with our souls, we need to deal honestly in business and all transactions. By relying on the Creator, rather than on our own schemes or business acumen, we express our trust in the Creator as the Provider of Life.

DAY TO DAY APPLICATIONS
OF THIS PRINCIPLE

Here are a few simple, day to day examples where we can be more careful regarding theft.

1 Small Time Theft: Most people are quite mindful not to steal, but unfortunately, sometimes people steal and are not really aware that they are stealing, for example, taking 'extra' office supplies or one too many candies from the dish of free candies. These may seem trivial but its actually theft. Similarly, sometimes a person may damage another person's property, say a fence that is located deep in forest, and the person will never know about it, and apparently it makes no difference to the person, but it is still theft. We must be as careful about not stealing a dollar as we are about not stealing a million dollars.

2 Time Theft: This occurs when employees are paid for time they did not actually work. Examples include taking excessively long breaks or spending work hours on personal activities like browsing social media. This too is theft.

3 Intellectual Property Theft: This is another example of a type of theft. This is the idea of using someone else's ideas, inventions, or creative works without permission or proper attribution. This of course includes copying software, music, or written content without paying for it or giving credit to the original creator.

05
A Deeper Perspective of Principle 05
RESPECTING OTHER PEOPLE'S PROPERTY

Just as we need to have respect for the bodies of others, as explored in principles three and four, we need to have respect for the property and dominion of others. In fact, true reverence for others automatically includes reverence for what they possess, and theft, whether literal or subtle, disturbs the unity and peace of interpersonal relationships, communities and societies. The right to own private property is essential for any safe, civilized society, community or family

WHAT WE OWN IS ON LOAN

As explored earlier, we must respect others' bodies and emotional lives, and we must respect our body and emotional life, as they are sacred gifts given to us by the Creator of All Life. By definition, this respect also extends to the property, information and ideas of others.

Although what we possess is not ultimately 'ours', and it only truly belongs to the Creator, what we have is a gift of safekeeping, and a loan. Our possessions are creations that we are given to look after in this world for the sake of the Creator. It is not a random coincidence that we have certain possessions and others have other possessions. These 'loans' were not given arbitrarily, rather intentionally and specific to each soul, each object necessary for that person's spiritual unfolding and actualization.

All the particular data of our lives, such as the parents we are born to, how we were raised, the place we live, the schools we have attended, the jobs we have had, the foods and the music we like — all these things in life, pass through our screen of vision because they are connected deeply to our soul. There is a soul connection between ourselves, our surroundings and all the objects we have owned. They are in a way part of us; they came to help us achieve our maximum spiritual, mental, emotional and functional potentials.

There is a deep underlying relationship between material and spiritual realities, and scattered throughout the world are 'sparks' of Divine Light which are connected to our soul. When we are attracted to specific people, places, objects, and foods, it is because we are seeking our Divine sparks. Within animate, vegetative and inanimate objects within our sphere of perception, these sparks are waiting for us to elevate them back to their Source Above.

We automatically gravitate towards the sparks that are connected to our soul's purpose and destiny. The mission entrusted to each of us is to reveal and release the sparks that are connected to our soul, by relating to them in ways that acknowledge their Creator and Sustainer.

Having this in mind allows us to live with more hope, optimism and freedom. True, sometimes we look around and see a broken and disjointed world filled with devastating hardship, loss, contention and conflict. Yet, within all the fragmentation around us, there are also intensely holy sparks that are made of the Light of Wholeness. Even within the apparent greatest darkness there is Light — there is wisdom, meaning, and purpose waiting to be sifted out, elevated and released. It is our task, our entrusted mission, to be co-creators with the Source to reveal that point of goodness, life, or hope.

OUR STUFF IS PART OF US

On a deeper level, everything in our life is an extension of our reality, and there help us grow and become more loving, expansive, open human beings. From the 'big' things in life, such as important interpersonal connections, and the 'smaller' things in life, such as the type of watch you have, all are part of who we are. Our 'self,' in the fullest sense, includes all of them.

Sadly, most people, do not have this integrated, wholesome perspective of life, rather, they see life as something happening to them, and the objects that surround them as more or less random. Because of this way of experiencing and thinking, as if they are holding life at arm's length, they can have much painful friction and resistance. If something challenging happens, the first question they ask is, 'Why did this happen to me?' But inherent in this type of question is the assumption that the things that are happening to them are not 'related' to them, that they are random and not inherently meaningful. If it seems things are thrown at us for no reason, they are felt as 'intrusions', and resistance to such friction is the root of pain.

This dynamic is also present within 'positive' events. Say a person makes a million dollar deal, wins the lottery, or finds their perfect spouse. When they live in a paradigm of separation, thoughts arise like, 'How did I ever deserve this? Is this a dream? Am I going to lose everything tomorrow?' Again, such thoughts come from a sense that what happens to them, the money they make, the objects they acquire, and even the people they have in their lives, are not meaningful parts of their lives and sparks meant for them to elevate. A more wholesome, unitive way of thinking and experiencing is that everything that happens to you, and everything and everyone who appears in your life, your spouse, parents, children, friends and associates, are all part of your essence. Just like you have legs, and they are part of 'you', everything in your sphere is part of your being.

Dismissing them as mere happenstance denies a basic tenet of faith: our actions have consequences and are related to perceived rewards and punishments. Instead of dismissing them, we can ask, 'What is the cause of this event?' However, even this suggests a subtle separation, as if the Creator is apart from Creation and guiding events from afar; we are still holding life at an arm's length.

The deepest way of living is from a place of total unity, in which the world and everything in it is a unified expression of Divinity. Nothing is separate from the Creator, and nothing is separate from us. From this perspective, the question is not, 'Why did this happen to me?' rather, 'What is the Creator telling me through this event?' Similarly, a thoughtful person who feels pain in his toe asks, 'What is my body telling me through this pain?'

LETTING GO WHEN NEEDED

We are deeply connected to the objects in our lives, and this is a real 'soul connection'. Each object presents an invitation for our Tikun / soul elevation through it. As stuff comes in and out of our lives, we may feel very connected at one point with a certain object.

If this connection is healthy, then after the purpose of our connection with that object has been achieved, we should be able to let go of the object with relative ease.

For example, imagine you had a favorite watch for many years, and one day it was lost. If you realize that your soul connection with this object was relative to the inner purpose and Tikun of having it in your possession, then, when it is no longer in your possession, you can intentionally let it go. You might grieve during that letting go process, but your faith will not be blemished, for you know that nothing is random, and that you have been shown that you no longer need a physical connection with that item.

THEFT IS TOXIC

All of this helps us understand the depth of the negativity of stealing. Taking from someone what belongs to him is in a sense 'stealing his soul'. And what the thief now holds in his hands is not just the object he coveted, rather a toxic energy — someone else's 'soul' as it were, is in his possession. What he has does not belong to his soul, it's like holding radioactive material in his hands. He may think he has gained something, when in fact he has lost something infinitely precious: his own soul and integrity. He brought into his home someone else's soul energy, which is out of place and burning to return to its true owner. Instead of releasing sparks to the Creator as he was meant to do, he has entrapped sparks, and these can only haunt him until they are returned.

THEFT IS ROOTED IN COVETING

Theft is rooted in coveting, not being happy with what we have, and looking at others, gazing longingly at what they have.

Unfortunately, many of us live with a sense of insufficiency and unmet needs, and our thoughts are often at the service of physical survival. This anxiety is, in part, a psycho-spiritual symptom of being surrounded by a capitalist society, in which advertising is designed to seduce and inflame our desires, and industry simultaneously creates a false sense of scarcity and lack.

In this terrible state of consciousness, everyone is living in everyone else's bedroom; everyone knows what everyone else has, where they live, where they vacation. This is because many so-called 'free people' actually live as slaves. They feel such a 'need' for the validation of other people, that they are 'enslaved' to them. They have given up their power of self-determination and identity, and rely on the outside world to tell them who they are, how they should behave and what to pursue. Their whole sense of what is good and noble, what has value and what does not, is based on what they see in others.

Our Creator intended to create a world of harmony and well-being, and we humans resisted it and replaced the Divine world with a world of loneliness, of deep lack and dissatisfaction.

As cravings are indulged, more and more desire is created. Newton's First Law tells us that bodies at rest tend to stay at rest, while bodies in motion tend to stay in motion in the direction in which they are moving, unless perturbed by an external force. As such, a desire fulfilled is not a desire quenched, rather, through the fulfillment of one desire, the person's vessel of desire only expands. As the vessel expands, so does the feeling of craving and need for more.

First a person feels dissatisfied with what they have, then they desire what someone else has. Then they can begin to covet it, meaning doing everything in their power, manipulating the other repeatedly to give or sell the object. This is because once a person becomes obsessed with what the other has, they may go to unimaginable lengths to obtain it, even scheming to rob it.

Interestingly, we only desire what we think we can attain and gain. You may desire to become a billionaire, if you see that someone else in your circumstances has done so: 'If he can do it, I can as well!' But if you are not a tall athlete, you will never even desire to become a professional basketball center. That goal has nothing whatsoever to do with you.

With a deeper understanding of life, you realize that what another person has is not yours, not meant to be yours, and is spiritually truly not in your reach. It has nothing whatsoever to do with you, and so you do not even desire it or imagine having it. In fact, it will produce distaste to imagine procuring something that is not part of your soul-purpose, because you sense that it will only be harmful. A wise person lives with greater contentment and less craving for what others have. On the contrary, a wise person is filled with gratitude for what he or she has, and enjoys a luxurious sense of contentment: "Who is truly wealthy? One who is content with what they have."

FOUR WAYS TO LIVE IN RELATIONSHIP WITH OBJECTS IN OUR LIVES

There are four ascending levels of approaching life in general:

1) Indulgence,

2) Avoidance,

3) Equanimity, and

4) Holy Re-embracing.

Indulgence. To impulsively indulge in and obsess about things is called 'unconscious action' and 'slavery'. This represents the human tendency toward the addictive, impulsive, slavish or mindless pursuit for 'more stuff', whether money, cars, gadgets, food or drink, academic degrees or the admiration of others, etc. For example, if, when you wake up each morning, you must drink coffee in order to function and feel well, then you are 'enslaved' to coffee. You are to some extent 'unconscious'. If there are certain foods you must eat, or if there are certain times of day when you must fill your belly or else you will be off-kilter or emotionally reactive, this suggests that you are living in some level of dependency. If you must get the newest iPhone to bring you happiness, then you are a slave to technology. A slave is someone whose life is dependent upon and fused with his master or his external surroundings, and their actions are sadly mechanical or robotic with little or no consciousness or free choice. Only in a relatively unconscious state can someone think they need a certain external 'thing' in order to gain happiness.

Avoidance. The first stage of breaking a psychological enslavement to external 'stuff' is to avoid, to refrain from indulgence. In the analogy of food, this may include fasting completely, avoiding only certain foods, or decisively separating oneself from over-indulging at any time. Fasting can be practiced for a day, or even for a few hours, such as skipping breakfast. A type of fasting can be practiced even while eating a meal. That is, if you find yourself indulging in self-centered eating or getting overwhelmed by your craving or appetite, simply put down the food, stop eating for a few seconds, settle your mind and body, and remember that you actually have the nutrition that you need. The same can be practiced with other objects of desire; choose to refrain from buying the newest gadget, or put away your smartphone or laptop every day for a few hours to disentangle yourself from subtle enslavement and unconscious behavior. Find other ways to train yourself to be free from mindless neediness and dependencies on unnecessary things.

Equanimity. The path of avoidance is a 'reaction' to unconscious indulgence, and therefore it is still entangled with indulgence. There is a third way that can open up to us once we have learned to refrain. In Hebrew this is called Hishtavus / equanimity. This is 'the way of transcendence' or equanimity. Once we are able to avoid grabbing for 'more', we should aspire to a spiritual plateau where we are always 'equal,' level-headed, conscious, balanced and free: 'I don't need anything outside of my-self to gain self-worth, sufficiency or happiness.'

Holy Re-embracing. This level represents holy enjoyment beyond equanimity. This conscious, grateful, unselfish pleasure is the blissful recognition of the Divine Essence within everything. It takes discipline and mindfulness to stay in this approach not sink again in the quicksand of physical indulgence, however it is important to develop this capacity for only from this place of holy re-embracing are we able to efficiently elevate the hidden sparks of spirituality contained within permissible objects.

There are still certain objects that are not to be embraced even from this elevated state of consciousness and freedom. We still may not take what is not ours, nor may we engage in destructive behaviors, or break any of the Seven Principles. The point is, having exercised our ability to refrain from indulgences and remain equanimous, we can then fully embrace and revel in what is rightfully ours and what is good for the soul. And from this level of inner freedom, we do not even desire what is not ours, for we are already independently fulfilled.

Here's how to get a glimpse of holy re-embracing: Put this book down for a minute and pick up an apple or another fruit in your hand. Pause for several seconds and settle your mind. Take a deep look and appreciate the profound beauty and intricate detail of the fruit's appearance. Take a deep inhale and allow the scent of the fruit to fill your nostrils. Then, draw the awareness of the Creator of this apple down into the act of eating by reciting a meaningful blessing with intention and passion. Say "Blessed are You, Master our G-d, Sovereign of the universe, Who creates the fruit of the tree". Now take a bite and feel the fullness of the Creator's majesty and glory extending all the way into the tastes and textures you are experiencing. When you eat this way, the total fullness and essence of your self becomes one, as it were, with the Divine spark within the fruit.

This is the deepest way of living — seeing and experiencing the full deliciousness of the Creator's light sparkling within every moment and within everything.

To reach this level of experience, whenever you are eating or looking to acquire something new, take a moment and consider whether you are eating or pursuing this thing because you objectively need it or because you are trying to fill an emotional void. Prior to taking your first bite of food, pause, become mindfully present and recite a blessing of gratitude to the Creator for creating this, and for giving you the opportunity to eat it. The act of reciting a blessing provides you with the opportunity to recognize what you are about to do. A blessing recited with proper intention opens you up to mindful presence and heartfelt gratitude, and this can help short-circuit eating from a place of craving.

In summary, to live a healthy, productive life free from subtle 'stealing', we ought to continuously reevaluate our relationship with the objects in our lives. We must ask ourselves from time to time: 'Am I the master of my objects or are they my masters? Contemplate whether or not you are able to acquire objects when you really need them, and when they can and should really be yours. Ask yourself whether you interact with any objects or substances in an unhealthy or unproductive way. Is the energy of addiction present anywhere in your life? When you lost something, did you obsess about it? When something became old and worn, did you still hold on to it? Do I 'steal' with my eyes by gazing at things that are not right for me to have? If I have taken something that is not mine to take, do I have the courage to admit it and give it back, if possible?

TAKEAWAYS /PRACTICES

- We automatically gravitate towards the sparks that are connected to our soul's purpose and destiny. The mission entrusted to each of us is to reveal and release the sparks that are connected to our soul, by relating to them in ways that acknowledge their Source and Sustainer. Before you pursue any pleasure, pause and ask yourself; am I indulging or being possessive? Is the object that I desire ruling over me, or can I step aside, refrain from indulging, feel a sense of equanimity, and if yes, then can I re-embrace it, without slipping into indulgence? Recite a blessing before eating food, thanking the Creator for creating it and allowing you to partake.

- If we learn to expect nothing from others, we will learn to appreciate everything and be grateful for whatever we receive. We should set times every day when we will focus on thanking the Creator for our lives and everything we have. For example, before we go to sleep, we should think over the day that just passed and specify several things that we are grateful for. When we awaken in the morning, we should thank the Creator for the new day.

- We are not asked to be grateful for every situation in our lives, but we are asked to be grateful in every situation.

06

SENSITIVITY TO ALL FORMS OF LIFE

J UST AS OUR RELATIONSHIPS WITH OTHER human beings should be loaded with loving respect and honor for the Divine Image within them, our honor ought to extend and flow to all forms of life. Our compassion and kindness should first fill our own souls, then flow to our family, community, and finally to the world at large, extending to every creation, including sentient animals and plants and even to inanimate objects and the mineral kingdom. We need to be especially compassionate to any creature that can feel or process pain.

The sixth spiritual principle and directive is focused upon the animal kingdom, and illustrated by the Divine command to refrain from eating a limb, nor any part, from a living animal. Part of the purpose of this principle is to stamp out all cruelty and to promote the kind treatment of animals. The human being is the model of compassion to all of Creation. We need to learn and re-learn to become the compassionate 'gardener' in the Creator's Garden. We, the children of Adam and of Noach, are responsible for the welfare of all Creation, and for our beautiful, sensitive planet, teeming with G-d given life.

The modern era's concern for animal rights and banishment of animal cruelty began some 200 years ago. But millennia before that, the Torah / Bible outlined various practices to ensure the safety and wellbeing of animals. Besides barring the consumption of a part of a living animal, the Torah prohibited other acts of cruelty, such as plowing one's field using animals of different species (Devarim / Deuteronomy, 22:10). Yoking different species together can cause physical or psychological suffering to one another. Similarly, when plowing a field, one is not allowed to muzzle an ox to prevent it from eating. This too causes tremendous stress for an animal — seeing food but not being able to eat it. There is also a general prohibition to cause undue stress to living creatures.

DAY TO DAY APPLICATIONS OF THIS PRINCIPLE

The principle of not consuming a limb from a living animal is part of not being cruel to animals and cultivating a sensitivity to all of life that surrounds us.

Here are some day-to-day examples of ways to learn to be more kind to animals.

1) Only Eat Animals or Parts of Animals that Were First Dead Before Cooking: Unfortunately, there are various culinary trends today that emphasize consuming fish and other animals as fresh as possible. This often results in practices where fish are immersed in boiling water and cooked alive, or even served alive. In some cases, limbs or parts of living animals are removed and boiled, causing immense suffering. All human beings should refrain from such practices to ensure humane treatment of animals.

2) Humane Practices of Pest Control: While no one wants pests in their home, and some can even be hazardous, besides being terribly uncomfortable, the way we remove them should reflect our sensitivity to their existence as living creations, created from the Source of all Life. It is certainly, for example, more sensitive to chase a bee out of your home than swatting it to death. This approach acknowledges that they, too, are part of the Creator's living creation.

3) Not Using Animals for Entertainment or Hunt: Locking up animals and forcing them to learn tricks for food is simply cruel. We should not use or abuse animals for our entertainment and amusement. Similarly, humans, just because they are more clever than animals, should not use their intelligence to hunt for sport, for fun and entertainment, causing unnecessary suffering before releasing the animal.

06

A Deeper Perspective of Principle 06

NATURAL INSTINCT TO LOVE, EXTENDED & OVERFLOWING

Essentially, this principle empowers us to live mindfully and with compassion, uprooting any perverse urge to act cruelly where one can, or wielding control and an underdeveloped sense of power over other creatures. As much as humanity may have a selfish urge to destroy, there is a deeper place within our souls, a consciousness that is rooted in Divine Love, which seeks to express unconditional love and care. In fact, as we are birthed and given existence from Divine Love, love is deeply rooted in who we are.

Again, we need to ensure that we are continuously broadening our circle of love from ourselves, to our family and community, to all human beings, to animals, and finally to all of Creation. In this sequence, we can eventually love universally without bypassing any stages of expansion or trying to replace love for people with love for other life forms.

It is important to remember some of the greatest cruelties ever perpetuated by man — a drama which played out in recent history — were planned and instigated by men who loved their animals dearly but were somehow able to murder a million and a half children. More recently, a well-known animal rights group penned a letter to a terrorist organization, requesting that when they blew up busses full of innocent civilians, that they should make sure no animals were hurt in the process. These stark examples of by-passing stages of love reveal the importance of embracing and spreading the Seven Principles in this time in history. We can consciously be part of the onrushing redemption, or we can deeply impede our own souls.

When love expands from the immediate to the more peripheral, it can eventually become overwhelmingly powerful, flowing effortlessly to all forms of life, carrying great blessing and well-being into the world. Still, in the immediate stages, love can take intense, committed work. It is not always easy to love oneself or one's parents, siblings or in-laws. One may need to start over again many times, and give without expectation of anything in return. However, ultimately, they will not jump to a superficial 'love for all creatures' or 'compassion' for people they have never met, rather their love will remain authentic even as it fills every ring of their experience.

Sometimes there may seem to be a tension between caring for one's family members and caring for the planet. One might prefer to serve a compelling social cause rather than spend time with his own children. But this tension is actually an inner dissonance, a call from one's soul intelligence which recognizes that 'loving everyone' means nothing if one is not yet able to love those who are closest.

The authentic insight that animals are precious, and that they carry the Divine life-force and express the infinite splendor of the Creator, is rooted in seeing your own preciousness and that of the people around you.

It is true that while animals are innocent and beautiful, humans are often full of ignorance and ugliness. Yet, our *Tikun* / soul perfection and challenge lie in loving our own human-ness and then extending that loving-kindness to other humans, and then to animals: "And you shall love 'your neighbor' (literally 'your friend', one who is closer to you) as yourself." This is not meant to condone human ignorance, nor does it mean to care only for your own community. It is a matter of sequence and the Divine design of authentic love.

BIBLICAL HEROES AND VILLAINS

Scientific studies postulate a relationship between a child's cruelty to animals and his criminal violence as an adult. Similarly, those who are described in the Torah as hunters of animals are villains, such as Nimrod and Esav / Esau. This shows us that hunting for sport is cruel, and that such cruelty spills out upon humans as well.

All those described in the Torah / Bible as caring for and shepherding animals are ethical and spiritual heroes, having extended their love to humanity, such as Yaakov / Jacob, Moshe / Moses and King David. Rivkah / Rebbeca was chosen to be the wife of Yitzchak / Issac because she showed compassion and sensitivity to animals.

Simply, we are meant to be representatives of our Creator, the All-Caring Source of Life.

THE ALIVENESS OF ALL OF LIFE

When we recognize that all Creation is lovingly infused with Divine life force, we will treat everything with sacred reverence. Certainly, we will have strong empathy for those creatures who have real feelings and emotions, even when they are less complex and sophisticated as humans. In this awareness, we will not even pluck a leaf from a tree for no reason. Today, science acknowledges that trees are 'social' beings, functioning within a social network, 'communicating' with each other, sharing nutrients, and even 'warning' other trees of impending dangers to their health.

Indeed, all living things are conscious, at least on some level. The ancient sages counseled us not to dishonor a loaf of bread, as if it could perceive us and have feelings. In following their model of sensitivity, we might even ask ourselves, as we are walking on pavement or gravel, 'What gives me the right to step on this?' We are not to abuse anything in Creation, certainly animals. We are allowed to eat animal meat when it is procured in the most humane fashion, but the question still resonates: what give us this right? Do I, with my actions and level of consciousness, really 'deserve' to pluck and eat fruit from a 'social' tree, to slaughter and consume the flesh of a sensate animal, to walk upon the ground that the Creator created, and to benefit from the Creator's own 'garden', which is this world? Am I living such a meaningful and noble life that so many precious life-forms will gladly give of themselves to nourish and benefit me? Am I living an elevated life in which even my eating and walking down the street is done in a holy, holistic manner?

BEING SENSITIVE TO ALL OF CREATION

The great spiritual master known as the Rayatz, the sixth Chabad Rebbe / soul guide, recounts that once as a young boy he was strolling the forest with his illustrious father, the Rebbe Rashab, the fifth Chabad Rebbe, when he said to him; "Son, look and see Divinity; even the smallest wavering of the tiniest blade of grass is vested with Divine providence!"

As he was walking and contemplating his fathers' lofty words, he absent-mindedly tore a leaf from a tree and began playing with it, tearing small parts of the leaf and dropping them into the wind. Seeing this, his father gently remarked: "Not only is every leaf vested with Divine life force, each and every leaf contains sparks of a soul that has descended to this world to find its correction and fulfillment.

"We have just spoken about Divine providence, and yet you disconnected a leaf from its source, and began twisting and tearing into little pieces and casting them into the wind. My son," he said softly, "how can you be insensitive toward a creation of G-d? This leaf, as all leaves, was made by the Creator, vested with His life force and set to accomplish a specific purpose. Like you, it has a body, and a life-force. In what way is the 'I' of this leaf inferior to your 'I'?"

This story is truly something to contemplate. And if we have expanded our love outward to the extent that we are sensitive to blades of grass and leaves, certainly we will not tear a limb, G-d forbid, from a living, feeling animal — nor steal from, kill or hurt a person, nor dishonor the Creator through speech or idolatry. We will honor the Giver of Life, and His aliveness which animates all things.

EXTERNAL BEHAVIOR AFFECTS INTERNAL MINDSET

Oftentimes, our external behaviors, such as acting sensitively toward other creatures, can transform us inwardly, causing us to become a more sensitive, attuned individual.

There are three approaches to understanding human behavior.

The first sees outward activity as reflecting a person's inward reality, and behavior in the world as flowing from the person's state of consciousness. As such, a negative inner state is never the source of a positive action, nor can a positive state of being produce anything harmful. According to this perspective if you act from anger, even if that action was technically positive, it would nonetheless be understood as essentially negative. If you witness an injustice, for example, and you feel anger toward the perpetrator of that injustice, any action you take based on that anger will be deemed negative. This approach could be called 'spiritual ethics'.

The second approach to understanding behavior is consequence-based: what matters most are the actions and not their intentions. If someone's actions are positive, such as helping to alleviate injustice, even if they are born from their anger or arrogance, they are nonetheless positive. It does not matter what your intention was — only the concrete result in the world defines the nature of the deed. This can be called pragmatic ethics.

The third, more holistic approach, and the one related to the Seven Principles, is both spiritual and pragmatic, unifying 'spiritual ethics' and 'pragmatic ethics'. It is a spiritual perspective, a heart space, which unfolds, perhaps paradoxically, within a context of pragmatic applications and laws. In this approach, our good deeds might emanate from a disturbed inner state such as anger at injustice — yet the process does not end with the actions. We know that the outward action, such as opening our hand to give a dollar to someone on the street, can actually open our heart and mind and create a positive inner state. Then, we can give again, this time from pure kindness.

Pragmatic ethics are valid because a good deed is a good deed. Yet, spiritual ethics are also important, because positive or loving consciousness does make the good deed more powerful. Even if we are feeling very negative, we can rely on the fact that our state of consciousness follows our actions. A positive deed can flow 'backward' from the outer world toward our inner consciousness and transform us from within.

Our ancient sages thus taught, "The heart follows the actions." Good actions help to create a good heart. Positive behavior opens us up to a more positive perspective. This is a secret to practicing each of the Seven Principles, as well as Teshuvah / returning to a good path in life, in general. In this, the sixth principle, when 'outwardly' we refrain from gratuitously harming or dishonoring animals and plants — even if we are merely following a principle and not truly flowing with compassion — we become more compassionate. We bring more sensitivity, attunement and goodness into the world, bringing both ourselves and the universe closer to redemption.

TAKEAWAYS / PRACTICES

- We need to ensure that our natural love and compassion for self and family extends outward to include all good human beings, then strangers and humanity as a whole, and then to the animal kingdom, etc. Note in your Seven Principles journal: a) Does your compassion extend to animals? For example, is your consumption of meat and animal products balanced or excessive? b) If you love animals or pets, observe yourself closely; is your love and kindness to them in any way a replacement for showing love and kindness to humans?

- "The heart follows actions"; good actions help to create an inner sense of lovingkindness. If you do not feel compassion towards all forms of life, perform an action that is aligned with compassion. Feel how that act resonates within, and how you begin to identify more as a compassionate person.

07

PURSUING JUSTICE & CHARITY

THE SEVENTH PRINCIPLE UPHOLDS all of the previous six and establishes them as communal and societal norms. The Divine truths distilled within those six principles are not meant to be embraced and practiced just by exceptional private individuals. "The world is established on three things: justice, truth and peace" — without systems of justice, truth cannot be widely upheld and there will be no peace. Only a society that follows fair laws is a peaceful society. A society that follows Divine laws of justice, truth and peace is a redeemed society.

Setting up a system of justice with courts of law and standards of social justice, includes appointing proper judges and enforcers in each and every community. By definition, such a system must treat all litigants equally, whether they be rich or poor, famous or infamous, foreigner or resident, honorable or less so, righteous or sinner.

Any injustice anywhere in the world is our problem, and we are responsible to ensure that righteousness prevails and that there are unbiased communal structures to serve this purpose.

One important practice of this principle is to pursue socially beneficial activities, such as giving charity, visiting the sick, honoring the elders, keeping one's word, not lying, and carefully practicing the other six principles and sharing them with others.

Ultimate judgment and true justice is the Creator's alone, yet, we are asked to be 'co-creators', so-to-speak, with the Creator in recreating and sustaining a hospitable world. When we do our part to help right the wrongs of society, uphold law and order, and secure justice for all, we are acting as 'co-creators'.

DAY TO DAY APPLICATIONS OF THIS PRINCIPLE

Upholding a justice system that is fair and righteous is our duty as a human being, as a participator, a co-creator, and the gardener of the Divine's Garden, which is this world. We must ensure that systems are in place to maintain law and order, and that these systems are founded on principles of justice and righteousness.

To make this happen, we need to take personal and collective responsibility and dedicate our money and time.

1) Standing Up Against Discrimination: If you witness someone being treated unfairly simply due to their social or financial status, skin pigmentation, social affiliation, or any other discriminatory trait, speak up, even if it is not popular. We need to speak truth to power.

2) Take Responsibility: If you see something wrong or an injustice, don't just sit there and complain. Take personal responsibility and try to do something about it. While individuals should take personal responsibility for the world, they should also support and uphold law and order, the foundations of any healthy and civilized society.

3) Charity of the Body: Upholding a just world involves giving charity, but charity is not limited to money. In fact, parting with your time and skills can be more impactful. For example, volunteering to mentor or tutor someone, whether it is a student struggling with their studies or a young professional navigating their career, is a significant form of charity. By providing valuable support and guidance, you can make a meaningful difference in their lives. Remember, there is always something you can contribute beyond money. Think about it and take action.

07

A Deeper Perspective of Principle 07

BETWEEN CHARITY AND TZEDAKAH

Souls are willing to descend from Paradise into this challenging world and live 70, 80, or G-d willing many more years, just in order to have the opportunity to do just one person an act of kindness or charity.

We usually think of 'charity' as specifically giving money, clothing or food to someone who needs those. The English word 'charity' comes from the Latin word 'caritas', which originally meant 'dearness', 'high in price' or valuable. Over time, this word came to imply esteem and love, and finally, altruistic love. Giving 'charity' is, in this sense, any act of altruistic love, generosity and goodness of heart.

Tzedakah is the Hebrew, Biblical term that people loosely translate as 'charity', yet the root of the word Tzedakah is Tzedek means 'righteousness' and 'justice'. This may seem confusing, since people think of 'justice' and 'charity' as opposites, and in English, 'justice' and 'charity' mean very different things. How is giving money to a person in need an act of 'justice'?

The truth is, an act of 'charity' is not just a 'praiseworthy' or 'kind' act, it is the right and just thing to do. We are obligated to give

Tzedakah to someone who needs it, because the money or food, etc., is meant to be given to them.

We may 'possess' objects or money, but we don't 'own' them. As creations, we possess lots of things, including our bodies, but we do not own anything. Everything is owned solely by the Creator of Everything. We are merely entrusted with possessions and nourishment; some of it is meant for us and our family, and some is meant for others who cross our path. If someone is wealthier than another, that is because he or she has been entrusted to distribute some of that wealth to the other. In other words, what you give to a needier person is rightfully theirs. It is only 'just' to give it to them.

Thus, Tzedakah, in Hebrew means doing what is right, whereas 'charity' implies giving others what is yours. To be 'charitable' is to assume that you are nice enough to give something that is 'yours'. To give Tzedakah means to be aware that the money you are giving to the poor has been offered to you as a gift from Above, to be kept in your trust until you are able to distribute a portion to its rightful recipient, the poor person.

If I give, thinking this thing is mine, earned through my hard work, but from the goodness of my heart I will transfer ownership to the other, I am subtly looking down on the other. If I give, knowing that what I possess is intended by the Divine orchestrator for someone else, I realize I am equal to the other, only my job right now is to give and the other person's job is to receive.

Tzedakah also establishes a relationship between the 'giver' and the 'receiver' and ultimately reveals a deep bond between them. There is a kind of cooperative 'teamwork' in performing the Will of the Creator in this transaction.

One reason some people hold back from giving is that they forget where their money came from. They figure they worked hard, and with their skill, experience and intelligence, they were rewarded with their income. But without grace and the Divine orchestration of all events, nothing would have happened. Tzedakah is given out of a higher vision, knowing that the Creator is involved in all giving and receiving, and that everything is for our Tikkun / soul purpose and elevation.

NOT HOLDING ONTO TOXIC ENERGY

Stealing, as we explored earlier, is to bring into your life toxic energy and to hold hostage someone else's displaced soul, as it were. Similarly, if we shy away from giving Tzedakah, we are holding onto money that does not belong to us, holding onto someone else's soul, to our own detriment. In fact, if a person holds on to the funds that are meant for a poor person, then he is subtly stealing from a poor person, and creating conflicting energy for himself. Even worse, his stealing their money is like stealing their soul, dangerously taking into himself energy that does not belong to him.

Even money that you inherit is also part of your 'loan', coming with the responsibility to give an appropriate portion of it to Tzedakah. Everything that is connected with you, your family, and what you possess is connected to your soul. If you attempt to hold onto something that is not given to you to possess, it brings a dynamic of disconnection into your life. It is like holding hot coal in your hands — it is in the wrong place, and you are not supposed to be connected to it in that way. Letting go of it is the *Tzedek* / right thing to do, and the quicker you rid yourself of it, the more relief it will give you. In this way, you should not procrastinate or put off giving until you have filled your own account with everything you need. When the opportunity arises, simply 'do the right thing.'

WE VERSUS ME

Returning to the distinction between Tzedakah and charity: 'charity', as in giving what is 'mine', is all about 'me'. Tzedakah, as in giving what is essentially connected to another soul, is all about 'we'.

In the 'me' paradigm, there is myself and another self: 'I' am doing 'you' a kindness by giving to you. There is an existential separation between us, and I am showing you love and care out of the goodness of my heart because I want to. I have all the power, and this is the classical definition of 'charity'.

In the 'we' paradigm, both 'I' and 'you' are creative expressions of the One Creator, and what I need to give you was yours to begin with. We are a kind of cooperative, benefiting each other. The opportunity to give Tzedakah is actually a gift from you. We share power.

In truth, the 'me' paradigm is the natural state of created beings. To acquire things and look out for oneself is as natural as breathing. It is what motivates us to work, to sharpen our skills and our thinking, to eat, sleep, procreate and keep ourselves out of harm's way. It is where independence is established. In this way, self-preservation is innate and healthy. On the other hand, it can become self-centered, aggressive and even abusive, if everything and everyone are approached as mere objects to be taken for one's own benefit or used for one's own pleasure.

The 'we' paradigm rides above our natural tendencies. It is a spiritual state in which each part recognizes its role within the greater whole. To love another person as yourself is to understand on the deepest level that they and you are essentially one. This is the realm in which inter-dependence blossoms. As we are parts of a larger whole, my wellbeing is dependent upon your wellbeing. On this level, we realize that we are a unity, a collective, limbs of one cosmic body, branches upon the Tree of Life.

A healthy 'me', healthy self-love, stems from knowledge that our lives have intrinsic meaning. We are each vested with a Divine purpose; we all matter and have something unique to the Tikun / perfecting of the entire world. This harmonizes with the 'we'. Just as I am special and unique and have a specific soul-purpose, so do you. When I can recognize the Divine Image and Divine purpose within myself, I can also recognize it in others.

TO GIVE IS TO RECEIVE

Based on 'natural' data, one would think that the more they receive, the greater their pleasure. Yet, the opposite is true. In fact, the most satisfying pleasure in the world is not to receive, but to give.

If we want to receive a great gift, the greatest gift we can receive is to give to others. A person experiences more inner joy and lasting pleasure from giving. For instance, when you walk down the street and drop a coin in a needy person's cup, if you're sensitive, you will realize that you feel better than you would if you found a coin on the street and pocketed it. The deeper reason behind this phenomenon is that by giving we are accessing our deepest selves and tapping into our inner spark of the Creator, our Divine Image, and thus revealing the Presence of the Giver of Life, within us.

We are a composite of body and soul. Our physical body is designed to be 'selfish', with a relentless desire to receive and accumulate, whereas our soul, our 'spirituality', is selfless. Our soul only desires to receive in order to give and share. Counterintuitively, the biggest gift we can give ourselves is to give to others and thereby tap into the limitless Source of Abundance. By giving we transcend our limited role as a 'creation' and enter into the infinite realm of the Creator. We become co-creators of a better world.

SEVEN PRINCIPLES OF RIGHTEOUSNESS

Just as the seventh principle provides a 'container' or structure that helps ensure the communal practice of the other six principles, the essential idea of Tzedakah / righteousness applies to each of the other six. It is only 'right' and 'just' to 1) worship and rely only on the one true Source of Life, 2) to bless and thank Him, 3) to refrain from taking the life of, or harming, humans — the ones who bear His image, but rather to benefit them, 4) to refrain from coveting or taking a partner that is not meant for you, but rather to protect the integrity of right relationships, 5) to refrain from taking anything that is not yours or meant for you, and 6) to give to animals and all creations of the One Source the compassion that is meant for them.

A person from any nation or background who carefully follows these Seven Principles, and continues to turn closer and closer toward the Creator is essentially a Tzadik / a 'righteous', holy person, one who exemplifies Tzedakah. The 'rewards' or benefits of such a life will be experienced in this world and beyond the grave as well. Most of all, such a person will have the 'reward' of knowing that he or she has given 'Tzedakah' to the Creator Himself, as it were. He or she will delight in the fact that they have given of themselves to help accomplish the Creator's cherished 'dream' and purpose for life on earth: to render this realm transparent to His Self-revelation, making this very world a "dwelling place" for the Infinitely Righteous One, with the coming of the final redemption — Amen / may this come to be, very soon and in our days.

TAKEAWAYS /PRACTICES

- Tzedakah is not an optional Mitzvah / Divine directive, nor is it merely to give from the goodness of your heart. Giving is simply the right thing to do. We should not let a day pass without giving to others, whether physical help such as money or food, emotional empathy, an encouraging compliment, or sharing spiritual inspiration.

- Remember, the greatest gift we can give ourselves is to give to others.

AFTERWORD
THE POWER OF JOY

WHILE CULTIVATING JOY IS NOT LISTED as one of the Seven Principles, it is the root and essence of all of them. Joy is the fuel that empowers you to perform good deeds and refrain from violating your conscience. In this way it is a meta-principle — as in the words of one of the great *Rebbes* / spiritual teachers: "Although there is no positive commandment to be joyful, and there is no sin in being depressed, yet elevated joy can bring a person to a level that no commandment can; and the depths of depression can cause a person to sink to a level that no sin can."

"Serve the Creator with joy!" (Tehilim / Psalms, 100:2). We are asked to see every moment as an opportunity to be joyful in a way that serves the Creator. In fact, happiness while performing a good deed can be considered an obligation, since performed without joy, it can actually generate negative consequences. When we do observe the Seven Principles with joy, that joy enhances and completes our observance.

Furthermore, being in a joyful disposition contributes to our mental and physical health, and nourishes our soul. Being joyful helps everyone around us, as well. Our states are contagious. When people walk around gloomy, annoyed, and with despondency as their face, not only is it not pleasant to be around them, but they pull down everyone else's state as well. When we are happy and wear joy on our face, we create a happier environment around us and we lift the spirits of everyone we come in contact with. In this way, when we are inwardly and outwardly joyous, we are serving G-d, serving the good in ourselves, serving others, and even the physical world around us.

While it is polite to say 'good morning' or 'good evening' to others in the street, it is also a moral imperative that as we encounter people throughout the day, we lift them up and not pull them down.

One should not think, 'If I am feeling sad or annoyed, who am I bothering? It is an internal issue.' The truth is, if you are expressing your bad mood, you are actually disturbing others around you, in addition to yourself. And if you are harboring negativity inwardly, you are probably expressing it outwardly in some way, and influencing your environment. If considering your own well-being is not sufficient, think about your obligation towards other people.

We may not always have the power, and mental or emotional stamina to 'think' ourselves out of a bad mood, but the core ability is always there. We always have free choice as to how we think about our lives. It is always possible to simply choose to cease, in any given moment, bemoaning our experiences. At the very least we can choose to 'act' joyfully, even if we do not feel it, as our internal moods are known to follow our external actions.

If you find yourself depleted of joy, surround yourself with more joyful, upbeat and positive people. Surround yourself with sounds of joy. When listening to joyful music, perhaps sing along, and maybe even clap or dance — notice how this changes your consciousness. If you are not feeling joy, acting joyfully can stimulate the feelings, as "our heart follows our actions." The mere act of choosing to smile can stimulate an inward response of joy.

The root of sadness is purposelessness and lack of direction. Many people who struggle with sadness do so because they lack a sense of cohesiveness and meaning in their lives; life feels like a collection of random or unrelated events. Joy, by contrast, stems from an acute awareness of purpose, mission, meaning and direction.

People who wake up every morning infused with passion for their mission and purpose, have a sense of inner drive, experience more joy in their day-to-day life. The nature of the human being is to work, to grow, to move, to evolve: "Man is born for toil" (Iyov / Job, 5:7). Therefore, when we work hard, when we have something in life that we want to accomplish, that is often when we feel most human, most alive and most joyful.

When we experience some payoff from our toil, there is joy. When we have exercised or cared for our body and feel stronger and healthier, or even when we have set financial goals and achieved them, a natural joy arises. When we realize we have grown emotionally and become more mature or wholesome, or when we have grown spiritually — all of this brings joy on its own level. Of course, the joy of working out pales in comparison to the joy of deep emotional healing, and certainly to that of sincerely serving the Creator, but each level of joy is integrally important in its own realm.

In the clarified state of keeping all Seven Principles, we know our purpose, our mission, what we need to do in this world, and how we can go about it. Chasing the next high, the next momentary excitement or relief, does not bring us lasting joy. We need the serenity of wholesome, Divine - centered living in order to rise out of that addictive cycle, to focus on what we need to accomplish in this world and how best to direct our energy and talents. The more we live with this settled, purposeful awareness, the more joy we experience in our lives.

Just as we experience joy when we are aware of our own personal purpose, deep inner joy also arises when we become aware that everything in life has purpose. There are no accidents or randomness in our own lives, but also throughout all Creation and all of history. There is a grand plan for everything and everyone in Creation, and the entire cosmos is inching toward redemption. Yes, there are apparent sets backs, descents, and regressions, but history is not just a straight line. From a wider viewpoint, the universe is indeed marching forward and upward, with humanity at the forefront. The movement is gradual, and sometimes it feels much too gradual, but nothing cannot reach its ultimate purpose. Individual and cosmic culmination are actually unavoidable. Joy is experienced when we are able to sense this positive evolution of all beings and all things, together as one.

TESHUVAH / RETURNING TO THE CREATOR WITH JOY

Adam and Eve brought depression and despondency into the world when they ate from the Tree of Knowledge, as well as the potential in their offspring — all of humanity — to violate each of the Seven Principles. Yet, we can create a *Tikun* / rectification in our own lives for the Tree of Knowledge. This is because 'sin' is not our 'original' state, rather the joy and clarity of living in the Garden of Eden. How can we return to that Edenic state now, in our lives?

The more we take responsibility for our lives, and for the ways our actions affect ourselves and others positively, the more we stimulate the evolution of the whole world into a state of Edenic joy, clarity and virtue. And the more we glimpse the gorgeously harmonious tapestry of life and its patterns, the more we see the Hand of the Creator — the more we are empowered to undo the curse of eating from that 'Tree of Sadness', and the more joy we can experience and radiate into Creation.

When we do something that is against our deepest nature it makes us feel heavy, or even 'guilty'. If we then continue to shame, blame or depreciate ourselves, the sense of heaviness can increase to seemingly unbearable levels. This is simply adding insult to injury. We need to ensure that our hearts and our homes, the sacred spaces we create, are filled with real joy, a sense of purpose, values, holiness, honesty and positive objectives. With a balanced sense of humor and lightness about our lives we can create a lighter and happier atmosphere. Then if life takes an unexpected turn, we can shake off any negativity and rebound more easily.

If you slip and fall, it does not help to lie there and beat yourself up about it. Perhaps instead you can see a little bit of humor in it, laugh it off, freely choose to get up, and then swiftly establish measures to prevent this mistake in the future.

There is a way of 'taking responsibility' that is heavy and burdensome, bringing with it a sense of self-consciousness and self-blame; 'I did such and such, how could I?' Beating yourself up for what you have done, or telling yourself that you are not such a good or righteous person, can become a self-fulfilling prophecy, for it re-enforces your negative vision of yourself, and thus your negative behavior. But there is also a type of responsibility that is serious yet it brings about a corresponding lightness of being: 'Yes, I made a mistake, I take full responsibility for my actions and choices — and I am open to immediately move on and be different, to begin anew and make better choices.' This is the type of responsibility that comes with Teshuvah / returning to the Creator, and returning to the great clarity and sanity of the Seven Principles. In this state of 'returning', we are free from any sense of blame or deflection of causality. We become authentically innocent and weightless, and we feel the magical joy coursing through all phenomena. We are 'returning' to the Garden while living in this world.

The first step to opening up to joyful Teshuvah is to simply accept whatever is truth in your life. "This is something that is real and I am really experiencing it right now. I am going to be present with this experience." Being present with an experience will allow you to start seeing some semblance of meaning within it.

So instead of resisting whatever it is that you are experiencing and saying, "This cannot be true. It is not real. I cannot be in this relationship, or this can't be happening to me," try simply being with what is. Often just being with the experience and saying, "This really is real, I actually am feeling this," can allow us to get something out of the experience we may not otherwise have gotten. This can come in the form of a realization, an inspiration, or a blessing.

Secondly, even if we have done something in the past that evokes regret, simply feeling regretful as an end unto itself is pointless and often counterproductive. Regret is only useful if it catalyzes one toward transformation, if not then our regret becomes a perverse form of self-indulgence.

Looking back on your life and saying, "I should have done this; I should not have done that," is meaningless. On its own what can possibly be the result of regretting past deeds, other than cultivating ill feelings toward oneself? What was done in the past is past, at this point it is mere memory. There is almost never a good reason to entertain ideas of 'could have' or 'should have'. These thoughts only germinate hostile feelings toward the one thinking them, and when people feel bad about themselves, they end up doing less for their current situation, not more.

On the other hand, the favorable aspect of regret is that it has a potential to inspire a review of the past and serve as a guide for the present. Though the past event cannot be changed, the way we tell the story about it can, and we can then come to see the past as a staunch protector of a more conscious future.

In order to do this, we need to emotionally detach ourselves from the past through objective observation so we can identify potential dangers that lie ahead if we were to select the same course of behavior. When used to inspire an examination of our past actions and intentions, the feeling of regret is positively charged. Transformation occurs when regret over a negative past becomes a beacon of light in the present that illuminates our path toward a more promising future.

In order to use regret in a healthy way, then, we must first clearly recognize what was wrong with our behavior and how our lives became misaligned from our soul. We should then accept upon ourselves a firm resolution for the future, and envision how much happier we will be when we are engaging in this resolution. Then, in the place where negativity and ill feelings of regret once suffused our inner space, we should generate a positive, life-affirming energy and let it permeate our consciousness, in a creative vision of our genuine growth and spiritual development.

When negativity seems unshakable, distraction can also sometimes work wonders. While warring directly against negativity may in fact only bolster it and add more fuel to the fire, one can often create a movement of positive Teshuvah by shifting our focus from negative thoughts to unrelated positive thoughts. Rabbi Mendel of

Kotzk once remarked that when the armies of Napoleon were surrounded by their enemies and on the verge of collapse, Napoleon initiated a great commotion away from the battlefield. The enemy turned and was caught off guard, and Napoleon and his men were saved. When we refocus our energies on some positive aspect of life, it can situate us in a completely different context and allow joy to enter the picture.

The most consequential aspect of time is now, the eternal present. Of course, 'what is' directly results from 'what was', yet the most empowered ingredient of teshuvah is the 'now'. In the 'now', we have the ability to transcend that which has been done in the past and to look at the present as a fresh starting point for a future filled with meaning and purpose and happiness. The power to behold the present as a clean slate, unmarked and unsoiled from the past, is available to us in this very moment.

Redemption — even greater than the experience of the Garden of Eden — is essentially already here, right now, if we will but open our eyes to it, embrace it with joy, and then act upon it.

TAKEAWAYS / PRACTICES

- Bring a touch of healthy, productive, anchored humor and lightness into your relationships or family life, and all your contacts. Being serious about our physical, emotional, mental and spiritual lives allows us to grow in all areas, but this should not become a fixed heaviness or gloom.

- Taking 10 to 20 minutes or more to thank the Creator for everything good in life will create an opening to soulful joy, and a sense of empowerment to full-hearted practice of the Seven Principles.

- Imagine that the world is balanced between fifty percent negativity and sadness and fifty percent positivity and happiness. Now consider that a single act of goodness, kindness or soulful integrity — even something small — can tip the balance worldwide, and create a cascade of happiness for all.

PARTIAL LIST OF BOOKS
BY THIS AUTHOR

THE POWER OF CHOICE: A Practical Guide to Conscious Living

RECLAIMING THE SELF: The Way of Teshuvah

THE GARDEN OF PARADOX: The Essence of Non – Dual Kabbalah

MEDITATION AND JUDAISM:
Exploring the Jewish Meditative Paths

BREATHING & QUIETING THE MIND

VISUALIZATION AND IMAGERY:
Harnessing the Power of our Mind's Eye

THE MYSTERY OF KADDISH:
Understanding the Mourner's Kaddish

UPSHERNISH:
Exploring the Laws, Customs & Meanings of a Boy's First Haircut

A BOND FOR ETERNITY: Understanding the Bris Milah

REINCARNATION AND JUDAISM: The Journey of the Soul

INNER RHYTHMS: The Kabbalah of Music

TOWARD THE INFINITE.

THE PURIM READER: The Holiday of Purim Explored

THIRTY – TWO GATES: Into the Heart of Kabbalah & Chassidus

EIGHT LIGHTS: 8 Meditations for Chanukah

PASSPORT TO KABBALAH: A Journey of Inner Transformation

THE FOUR SPECIES: The Symbolism of the Lulav & Esrog

THE JEWISH BOOK OF LIFE AFTER LIFE

MYSTIC TALES FROM THE EMEK HAMELECH

INNER WORLDS OF JEWISH PRAYER:

WRAPPED IN MAJESTY: Tefillin – Exploring the Mystery

SOUND AND VIBRATION: Tuning In to the Echoes of Creation

SECRETS OF THE MIKVAH: Waters of Transformation

THE MYSTERY OF SHABBOS: Shabbat Rediscovered

MURMURINGS OF MAJESTY:
The Mysteries of the Shofar & Rosh Hashanah

A LIGHTNESS OF BEING: Your Guide to Yom Kippur

THE JEWISH WEDDING:
A Guide to the Rituals and Traditions of the Wedding Ceremony

THE SPIRAL OF TIME:
Unraveling the Yearly Cycle & Rosh Hashanah

THE MONTH OF NISAN:
Miraculous Awakenings from Above

THE MONTH OF IYYAR:
Evolving the Self & The Holiday of LAG B'OMER

THE MONTH OF SIVAN:
Balance & the Art of Receiving & the Holiday of Shavuos

THE MONTHS OF TAMUZ/AV:
Embracing Brokenness & Transforming Darkness

THE MONTH OF ELUL: Days of Introspection and Transformation

THE MONTH OF TISHREI:
A Time of Rebirth and Upward Movement

THE MONTH OF CHESHVAN:
Navigating Transitions, Elevating the Fall

THE MONTH OF KISLEV:
Rekindling Hope, Dreams and Trust

THE MONTH OF TEVES:
Refining Relationships: Elevating the Body

THE MONTH OF SHEVAT:
Elevating Eating & The Holiday of Tu b'Shevat

THE MONTH OF ADAR:
Transformations Through Laughter & Holy Doubt

THE HAGGADAH: Pathways to Pesach and the Haggadah

ILLUMINATED SOUND: The Baal Shem Tov on Prayer

AWAKENINGS: Drawing Life from the Weekly Torah Reading

PRESENCE AND PROCESS: Life in Balance

CONTEMPLATION & DEVEIKUS:
Hisbonenus: The Meditative Path of Chabad

EMBRACED IN DIVINE SPACE:
The Festivals of Sukkos, Hoshanah Rabba & Simchas Torah